| Advertising

Extol the benefits of the product.

| Business

Diverse, Sustainable Revenue Streams; Efficient Resource Use.

| Choragus

Leader of the chorus; person officiating at festival.

CHORAGUS (Volume 1: Greetings from Astoria)
©2007 A.M. Sherwin   All rights reserved.

PUBLISHED BY HAPPY MEDIA, LLC

Happy Media®

www.happymedia.com

help@happymedia.com

800.813.8952

Happy Media, the Happy Media logo, WHOMP, Domainsmith, Skillmax, Good Homes, and Access Road are registered trademarks of Happy Media. Portions of the material in this Volume have appeared in Weekly Update (www.weeklyupdate.com), Daily Examiner (www.dailyexaminer.com), Astoria Expresso, eBusiness Journal (www.ebusiness.ca), and other properties.

Cover designed by Angie Shearstone (www.angishearstone.com).

A.M. Sherwin is represented by Author's Agent Representation (authorsagent.com).

ISBN: 978-0-6151-3827-5

Friday, December 16, 2005

Just now, I used the ATM at the bcp bank near my home in Astoria. I was on my way to pick up the laundry. I'm out of socks. I swiped my card for entry, and proceeded to withdraw my $100. I threw out my receipt, remembered my card, and attempted to open the glass doors of the vestibule.

As it turns out, they were now magnetically sealed. Hmm. And me once again without my phone.

Luckily, I was able to flag down a passing pedestrian, and managed to give him the international symbol for "Please swipe a card, any card, into the machine. So that it will let me out, as it has no right to keep me here. On a Friday evening."

Problem solved. But really...you've got to be f***ing kidding me.

Oddly, this was the second time in 3 days that I've had problems with locked doors. The first time, however, it was entirely my own fault.

posted by ams at 6:42 PM

HAPPY MEDIA
10TH BIRTHDAY EDITION

CHORAGUS

Volume 1: Greetings from Astoria

By A.M. Sherwin

CONTENTS

Suggested Soundtrack:

Trying your Luck (The Strokes)

Santeria (Sublime)

All of the Above (Big City Rock)

Blame it on Me (Barenaked Ladies)

The Lakes of Pontchartrain (The Be Good Tanyas)

Ask Me Anything (The Strokes)

Youth (Matisyahu)

Cast No Shadow (Oasis)

Top of the World (All-American Rejects)

Helpless (Crosby, Stills, Nash & Young)

Get Over it (OK Go)

A Little Less Sixteen Candles (Fallout Boy)

Glory Box (Portishead)

Judith (A Perfect Circle)

Only in Dreams (Weezer)

Exit Music for a film (Radiohead)

Introsurf

It's nice, having put myself out to pasture while I'm young enough to enjoy it. I remain the hardest working man in Internet Business. I mow, I rake, I shovel, I hike. I play a lot of golf. I read. Most days I take a walk into town. To the library or the little bakery, or to the drugstore for a day old paper. It's quiet. There's a lot of nature, but we're still quite close to the city.

Do I miss the bustle, and the hustle? Do I miss the racing rats? No. I drink less whiskey up here in the country, and I feel less stress.

There are three things on the first page of this book. A brief discussion of them will, I suspect, give the reader a clear understanding of the intended purpose of the pages that follow.

a. This book is, above all else, intended to encourage you to support Happy Media. By visiting our web sites, and purchasing our products and services. I intend to encourage you by extolling the benefits of our products and services. For example: Our service packages offer better value, dollar-for-dollar, than any similar provider.

b. I believe that the principles we've used to build our business are Basic Business Fundamentals, applicable to business in general. These are fundamentals are, in short: Diverse, Sustainable Revenue Streams; Efficient Resource Use.

c. This is Volume 1 of Choragus. The Choragus was the leader of the Chorus, in Ancient Greece. Ideally, that's what Happy Media would be. The agent that gives voice to the chorus. I think we're well on our way. If we can accomplish as much in the next 10 years as we have in the first, we'll get there.

What is Choragus?

Volume 1: Greetings from Astoria is ultimately a series of loosely connected essays, united by context and narrative voice, so feel free to skip around and read what you like, at your leisure. This is my two cents, in print rather than on your screen. The Chapter titles refer to Clients, Projects, Services, or something else related to life, business, sport, or New Jersey.

One some essential level, this is a book about business. With some sports, current events, minor-key drama, and *literary aspirations*, just to keep things flowing properly.

The pages that follow will feature anecdotal and purely circumstantial evidence of the superiority of our business model, commentary (solicited and otherwise) on a wide range of subjects, embarrassing stories of hubris, as well as case studies and highlights from our most popular projects.

Every day of our lives, we Happy Media people publish electronically. Even though many of us have print media backgrounds, the sort of editing required of a print publication of this length is not our everyday task. As such, anybody finding formatting errors in this edition please let us know, so that we might fix them. You'll get a Happy Media sweatshirt for your trouble.

It's been a long time since I've had the opportunity, let alone the inclination, to do some extended typing. I'm a little rusty, but if you bear with me I think you'll enjoy the story that's in between these pages.

I'm hopeful that we'll be able to do a lot with this most recent incarnation of Choragus. This brand serves as an ideal metaphor for The Happy Media Network and its properties, its guiding principles and core competencies. It's a shining example of perfect vertical integration.

On the wall opposite my desk is a bookshelf. On it are four books written by my grandfather, 50 or so years ago. So ultimately, in this long-anticipated age of on-demand printing, Choragus will be where you will be able to find all of Happy Media's most serious thoughts. We have quite a few voices to share, and I doubt that mine will be the loudest.

What is Happy Media®?

We're often asked…what exactly is it that you do? Our Elevator Pitch has evolved from a page long calculus to three simple sentences. Happy Media owns and operates a network of Internet Businesses. The company provides corporate, creative, internet, and marketing services to a wide range of clients. We also do a lot of Community Stewardship work.

I'd like to think that I speak for a whole bunch of us when I say that we were the last company anyone would have pegged to have gotten it right. But here we are…and here you are, reading our lovingly produced product…go figure.

A Happy Media is a way of life. It's what people are talking about when they write about "the changing workplace", and telecommuting, and the portable worker (www.portableworker.com). In corporate-speak, it's the Action Plan for a better way of life. And the thing is…it works.

I am not a practical person. That's the first thing you must know, as I begin to talk about starting, building, and running a business. I have some innate skills, and some others I've developed and cultivated…but a practical nature is not one of them. But I am a grinder. The things that I can do well, I can do for hours and hours and days and days until something stops me. In the meandering course of a day, I write some copy for a client web site, then create a new brand name, then migrate some data to a new system, then do some networking, then send out our newsletter, then help a non-profit client with a fundraising issue, then check the traffic stats of our paid parking properties, then build some simple graphics, then update some client information, then send out and pay some invoices. And I can do this day after day after day…which is how we got here, 10 years down the line.

Team Happy Media 2007

You may have recently read some breathless declarations of what business looks like in this new millennium. Well, guess what? That's Happy Media. For a while, we had to maintain the illusion that what we do is somehow similar to the way business was run in decades past. And thus, for 6 or 7 years, we had a large, fairly traditional office. But after nearly 10 years, in the space of 6 months, we turned that on its ear. And now, we enter 2007 with a fully decentralized human resource infrastructure, we're stronger and more productive than ever before.

This company started in a small apartment. We eventually moved to a larger one, then to suite of offices, then another suite of offices, and now, we're a few essential personnel (mainly myself, our Director of Operations Matt LaRose, and a few project level managers scattered across the East Coast), bolstered by a handful of world class outsourced essential service providers (AT&T, Peer1, eNom, Intellicontact, GoDaddy, Ring Central, Paypal), and a small army of interns, freelancers, friends, family, and colleagues.

Here's a picture of headquarters, in the Winter of 2006, on the day we had it inspected. It's a nice house. Old (1880) and in a great, historic neighborhood close to town. The office is on the back of the house, above the garage, near the kitchen, with a separate entrance. We've got all the PCs and Broadband we could need…and poor cell phone reception, which improves productivity. In our capability testing, we've found that our current bandwidth resources rival or improve upon those of most commercial offices.

In Astoria, the hall and the roof were just about our only source of recreational space, with the exception of the Big Space (more about this later). Here in the lovely Litchfield Hills, our yard has a nicely spaced wiffleball field, golf ball chipping area, and front hedges that in Summer are just about ideal for stopping a soccer ball.

The Happy Media Network

Simply put, we own and operate 250 or so small businesses. Some of them generate revenue for us, some of them provide other resources, and some we sell.

There is not another Network out there like ours. When you combine the web sites we own and operate with those of our many partners, clients, and related entities, what we have is a very large, very loose group of mostly like-minded folks...most of whom don't even know each other. For example, our Online

News Center, Daily Examiner, has many people who have written for it who I have never met, and who have never seen the inside of a Happy Media office.

Happy Media® is also a Business Developer and Service Provider. Our network of people speak English, Spanish, Burmese, French, Russian, Polish, Slovak, Czech, Latvian, Bengali, Urdu, Hindi, Mandarin, Cantonese and other languages.

The most robust Network of its kind, The Happy Media Network represents a fundamental advance in the evolution of business. Our enterprises share non-industry-specific resources, in order to achieve economies of scale that would be unavailable to them as independent operators. The Happy Media Network is a constantly evolving entity, much akin to a Large Metropolitan Transportation System. Niche offerings radiate outward from several central hubs. These hubs combine with our diverse beta-stage properties to offer a remarkably broad selection of products, services and information.

The History of Happy Media

Happy Media was founded in 1997, and the origins of the Network date back to 1985, when a young A.M. Sherwin wrote his first Press Release, for HWH Enterprises (hi guys!). I then went on to write for several popular and unpopular publications, including The NY Daily News and The Berkshire Record.

Our business model builds sustainable, fiscally sound enterprises from the ground up, through maximum resource-use efficiency and revenue stream diversity. Happy Media's history is marked by innovation, sweat and productivity under sometimes less-than-ideal circumstances.

For a more in-depth look, visit MEDIAHAPPY (www.mediahappy.com), an ongoing retrospective of all that has been, is, and will be Happy Media. You'll find a fairly comprehensive Retrospective, Timeline, and a Collection of funny looking sites from our early years.

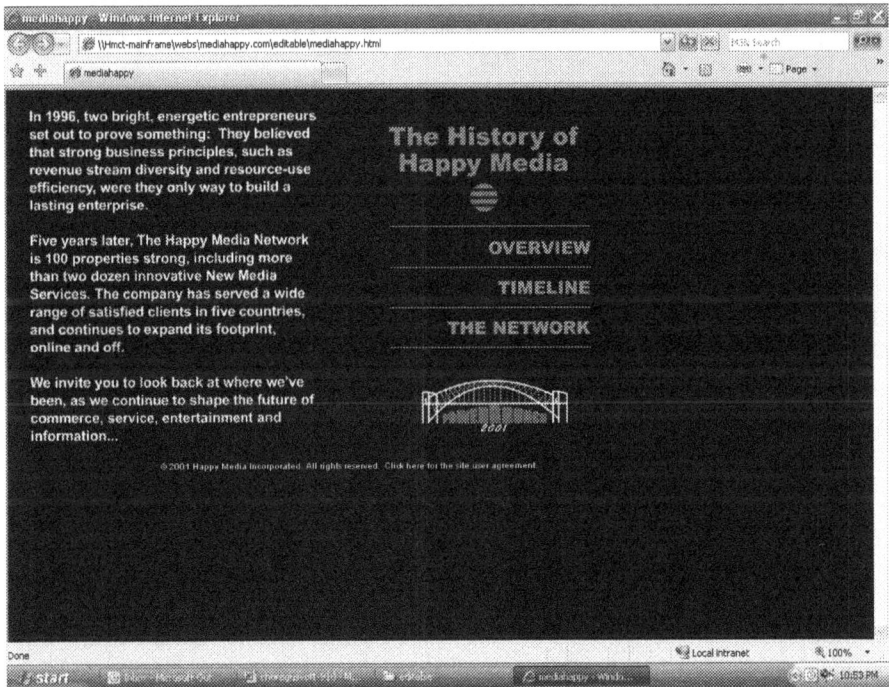

Actually, um, don't. Mediahappy is one of the many self-referential sites we've let fall into disrepair. This book aside, we rarely toot our own horn. Mostly we just send our newsletter,

Weekly Update, out 25 or 30 times a year. And we disseminate a few postcards, brochures, sweatshirts and mugs to our faithful, and total strangers, when we have the funds to so.

In Business? Let Us Help You.

We've worked with a truly astonishing range of people and organizations. From telecom giants and artists and writers to shipping companies to theatre companies to historical archivists. This allows us to bring, in addition to a truly unrivaled range of services, a unique personal perspective to any sort of enterprise. Contact us today to let us starting helping you, too.

On November 13, 2006 we announced the launch of the brand new home of our Commercial Operations, the Small Business Internet Ventures site Version 1.1 (www.sbiv.com). This site has a comprehensive alphabetical listing of more than 230 of our top properties, as well as links to handy resources for any modern business.

From time to time, when we receive serious offers, we sell one or two of our properties, in an effort to monetize our assets for the long-term fiscal health of the network.

For example, in late November, we sold fastclips.com and luxurysuite.com to private buyers, for approximately $15,000. This allowed me the opportunity to finish this book, while acquiring and beginning to build more than 20 new web ventures, including Tasty Fries (tastyfries.com), an entertainment site, Golf Clan (golfclan.com), a golf networking site, and bizop.org, a resource center for our many Non-Profit clients.

We've forged some essential principles and commandments for the modern internet business, or for that matter, any business. The Happy Media business model is predicated on these fundamental principles.

***

FOR IMMEDIATE RELEASE

Registrant.org Leaps to the Front

December 27, 2006 (Litchfield, CT) The Happy Media Network (www.happymedia.com) today announced the launch of www.Registrant.org, a new platform that will allow Community Groups to access cost-effective Web Site Services.

"This is the most exciting advance in Non-Profit services in years," said Happy Media Executive Director Adam Sherwin, "Registrant.org goes right to the heart of our strengths: internet services for non-profits, community groups, small businesses, and individuals."

With this latest property, Happy Media now offers all eligible organizations (also including education organizations, sports groups, and arts practitioners), and its existing stable of Community Stewardship clients, superior products, services, and support.

The company hopes that this new location, www.Registrant.org, will raise accessibility for groups that currently don't know where to turn for corporate quality service.

"We've partnered with the industry leader in value pricing to offer a full complement of services, including Domain Services, Web Hosting, Email, SSL, Ecommerce and more", said Mr. Sherwin, who also releases his first book, Greetings from Astoria, in early 2007. Happy Media already services a wide range of clients, from Arts Groups and Human Rights Organizations to Historical Societies.

Astoria

It's hard for me to talk about Astoria without getting a bit misty. My time there was monumentally productive, and productivity generally makes me happy. I made many friends there, and continue to work to make it an even better place.

This whole Happy Media thing started in Astoria. Two crazy kids in a tiny little (technically a 2 bedroom…but it couldn't have been more than 450 square feet) apartment, trying to carve out a little slice for themselves.

Out in that part of Astoria, it sort of feels like the end of the earth. You can see the fire about ½ mile away, out in the Long Island Sound, up 100 feet in the air from some sort of CONED Energy facility. Plus, we're pretty close to Riker's Island out there.

After 2 years in that apartment, in 1999 we moved to a slightly bigger and better one, at the corner of 34th and Broadway in what I think of as the heart of Astoria (30th Avenue officially claims that title). And on January 3, 2000, Happy Media moved into a suite of offices in the Thomas M. Quinn Memorial Building, about 150 yards away.

Over the next six years, this suite of offices in an historic building would be a blessing, a burden, a clubhouse, a wiffle-ball court, and a cafeteria.

We've had the pleasure of working with local businesses ranging from bars and restaurants to arts groups, schools, business associations, deathcare service conglomerates and many, many others. We continue to work with the Astoria Performing Arts Center, Greater Astoria Historical Society, Steinway Street Business Improvement District and other groups.

Not long after we moved into the Quinn Building, and we met a young Zine Team, who did a profile about us for their 6th Month Anniversary Edition of "Astoria Expresso".

We've gotten some good and interesting press over the years, but this remains my favorite, despite numerous glaring inaccuracies.

PEACE, LOVE AND "HAPPY MEDIA"

by Justina Williams

Some of HM: l-r: Kevin, Matt, Nico and Dallas

Sitting in their office above Quinn Memorial Funeral home, the two creators of new Astoria internet company "Happy Media" aptly demonstrate the balanced forces which led to the networks creation — and burgeoning expansion. The slow-talking, but deceptively fast moving Adam Sherwin is continually exiting and reentering the room, pausing only to grab a digital voice recorder whenever he comes upon an idea which he is particular pleased with. Meanwhile, his partner — in life as well as business -- Catherine LaRose remains at her computer interjecting occasionally and reigning him in whenever he appears at risk of accidentally pursuing any speeding train of thought out the fourth floor window.

One wouldn't ordinarily peg a 24 year-old college drop-out (Adam, Simon's Rock of Bard) and a 23 year-old English lit graduate (Catherine, NYU) as poised for world domination. And indeed, the duo themselves decry the possibility - "At that point your business principals are no longer an issue - it's just how much you're willing to do to the other guy," but in the parallel reality that technology has created, Happy Media could very possibly become a contender. Three years after its inception the corporation boasts nearly 30

>>>>>>>>>

June 2000   11   *exPRESSo*

clients, primarily foreign, and is in the process of finalizing work on the creation of an additional 150 "brands."

The "brands" are actually separate companies which function under the Happy Media umbrella and are owned by the parent company — and offer a vast array of services. Up and running already are "Domain Shark," (domain name creation and registration), "Whomp! Sports" (sporting goods) "Good Homes" (country wide real estate listings) as well as "Unigent" (website hosting and developing.) Currently in creation are additional brands ranging from "Choragus" (content for websites and publishing) to "iBodega" (your corner store on the web.)

Adam explained that the Happy Media Network differs from seemingly similar "internet incubating" companies in that "rather than buying it piece by piece, we're building it from the ground up. So we're able to build it much more efficiently.

"The reason that it can be difficult to grasp is that no one has ever done it before — set out to create 150 different other companies."

He added, "We haven't blown up yet - in any sense of the word - but what we have done is undergone an uncommon level of growth in terms of the speed with which we've gone from a two person operation set up in someone's living room, to a 12-20 person company with a couple good band names, a brick an mortar footprint in several states and a very significant and rapidly expanding electronic footprint."

The son of a former writer for The Daily News and grandson of a news editor for The New York Post, Adam has been media oriented, and bit by the entrepreneur bug since the beta stage of development — fourth grade, when he started his elementary school's newspaper. Though some projects have been more successful than others - Happy Media's first incarnation was as an underground zine "Read This," which both Adam and Catherine describe as "Terrible, puerile if not infantile. The only strategy we had was to head into the city with a messenger bag and unload them onto various students , passerby's and book stores."

Though that project was soon superseded by the need to pay rent, Adam was soon plotting again, this timehe relyied on skills he'd nurtured while writing articles on programming for The Daily news and various tech magazines, supplemented by Catherine's past as na adolescent video game fanatic.

Prior to moving to Astoria the two nurtured Happy Media's early growth, though working additional jobs they managed to create domain names or do freelance work under the Happy Media logo in their free time. Eventually they made enough to focus on the project. "The philosophy has been 'If we can get through the next six weeks, we won't have to worry — we'll built than worry about the next six weeks,' and it's worked really well," says Catherine, who adds, "It kind of makes me nauseous, I'm not meant for that insecurity -- but everyone else thrives on it."

None of the staff, who frequently work weekends and late into the night, are over 25. Indeed Catherine is the only company member boasting a degree, except the Vice President of Creative Development of whom Adam muses, — "has some sort of masters."

However the lack of paper propriety has done little to bar their growth which feeds largely off adrenaline, enthusi-

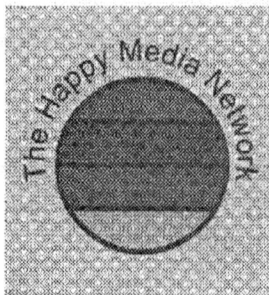

asm and team spirit. While Catherine notes that Adam is a great motivator, he gives equal credit to the pickup games of baseball and basketball played amid the offices, adding "We don't take ourselves too seriously — though we take the work very seriously."

To whit, the site for Happy Media brand "Its Not Just Any Corporate Identity Service," hints to its clients, "Talent is cheaper than table salt. What separates the merely talented from the successful is hard work," — Stephen King.

And while the newly inhabited office space is sparsely furnished, and they're not yet raking in the spoils of their labor — the company is pleased to note they have no debt. "We didn't ask anyone for help. And since we can't spend money we don't have, we have to make it before we spend it," said Adam. A fact he adds carries over to their customer service. "We deliver value by making the most use of all possible resources. Having been poor for so long we have proven that we can do more with $1 than anyone else can."

Meanwhile they have no plans to relocate, and the two note, "We've lived in Astoria since 1997, and ever since being here the company has grown and flourished. We really like the area — the fact that it's still a neighborhood, that we know the name of the guy in the hardware store — Bobby Shapiro."

■

At the moment, here in CT, there really isn't a Happy Media scene like we used to have back at the Quinn Building. 3 or 5 or 12 of us, typing and talking, and playing wiffleball, and running through the halls of the funeral home. We're at the early stages of converting the Archive Annex (semi-attached garage) into what I think is going to be the nicest work spot we've had yet for our interns, friends, and clients. When we're finished, we'll have the perfect space for the company's long term development. 8-12 networked machines in a bucolic versatile indoor/outdoor space close to town. Stay tuned. Come visit.

I have a very nice office in the back part of my home off the kitchen, and an archive annex (garage) out back. We also have professional space available for our use in just about any city we might be.

We retain the small army of friends, colleagues, writers, designers, programmers, interns, clients, and associates. We're just all spread out across the East Coast, the West Coast, the Middle, Canada, and frequently Europe and Asia, depending on the season.

Although, just yesterday (10/09/06), we did receive an inquiry from a young man from just down Route 202 in Torrington. He's looking for an opportunity, which is almost always how people find us. This one doesn't seem to have too much English, but that's also not his area of interest, and thus it's irrelevant.

Greetings,

 My name is Alan and I am a college student that is currently trying to get my BS in graphic design, I have my associates in Fine arts. I was wondering if Happy Media has an opening or maybe an apprentice ship or an internships? Thanks and have a great day.

No, these days Happy Media Headquarters is my office alone. Plus the servers in Atlanta, the registrar in Maryland, the home offices in Astoria, Jersey, Maryland and beyond. My current office is about the same size as my office was in Astoria (about 300 square feet), but it's got more windows, and by the time you read this, some new Bamboo flooring we acquired at the Home Depot.

The major upside to all this is severalfold: Happy Media's expenses are at a 6 year low, we have better, more up-to-date online infrastructure (servers) than we've had in quite some time. Just about the only project that's taken a major hit is Entry Draft, and I'm certain that that is temporary.

Entry Draft is our Innovative Internship Program. You'll hear some interesting young voices from it in a few pages. It's part of The Juggernaut, Happy Media's Community Stewardship Arm. We've had a lot of fun over the years, working with students from every imaginable background, and hopefully sending them off a little better for the experience.

To be honest, as I mentioned earlier, the only aspect of our business that's declined as a result of our move to the country has been Entry Draft. So if you're in CT, and you want to receive school credit, or valuable portfolio material, drop us a line anytime.

Community
Stewardship

If you represent a Community Group or other Non-Profit that needs corporate quality new media services, visit us today at www.juggernaut.org. We provide pro bono and discounted services to arts groups, environmental organizations, schools, historical interests, human rights groups, and other Community Positive Organizations.

We're committed to being positive contributors to our community, both online and off, both locally and globally. There are so many things each of us is capable of doing for our fellow people, every day, that there's just no reasonable excuse for not doing something.

We also believe very strongly in walking the walk. What follows are a few casual case studies of some of the organizations with which we've had the pleasure of working. We've done a wide variety of things for these groups, but one thing unites them, in my view: they all represent the sort of thing I have in mind when I go on (and on) about Community Stewardship. These are community positive groups that have grown organically, and satisfy an otherwise unmet need in their community. For the most part, we provide these groups with internet services (hosting, domain, web mastering, etc), consulting services, and analysis. As soon as our corporate side (read: bank balance) catches up to our non-profit side, we hope to make greater and greater contributions as our resources allow.

A.S.A.P (text from www.africansolutions.org)

ASAP aims to mitigate the impact of HIV/AIDS on Orphans & Vulnerable children in South Africa by building the capacity of our partner Community Based Organizations. ASAP regards these Community Based Organizations as strategic partners in the HIV/AIDS epidemic, in our effort to provide sustainable care for Orphans & Vulnerable children through nutrition, education, medical and emotional support.

ASAP believes the best strategies come from the communities themselves and the women who have responded voluntarily to the crisis of AIDS orphans. We support and promote the effective programmes that they have developed.

ASAP recognizes a responsibility to help these groups develop their solutions slowly, from the ground up.

Through the collaborative administration of incremental grants, ASAP ensures accountability by training in basic accounting skills and monitoring and evaluation techniques. These Community Based Organizations and their network of women are scaling up and replicating their holistic models of care in the face of ever-increasing numbers of orphans & vulnerable children.

ASAP equips women in neglected rural areas with the technical skills they need to realize their dreams. ASAP empowers women by providing them with opportunities to learn from the expertise and experiences of one another, using the intellectual resources of our CBO partners and indigenous teachers and facilitators.

ASAP believes that any change and intervention must stand in organic relationship to what the people on the ground are already doing. By linking Community Based Organizations with local government agencies, we are helping to secure sustainable resources for the future of these rural communities. Because of their close proximity to villages and households, this vast network of women and their existing infrastructure provide a valuable entry point into communities that are often not reached by the mainstream HIV/AIDS programmers.

ASAP supports orphans and vulnerable children by strengthening the extended family and support structures through community based intervention.

Temporary Distortion

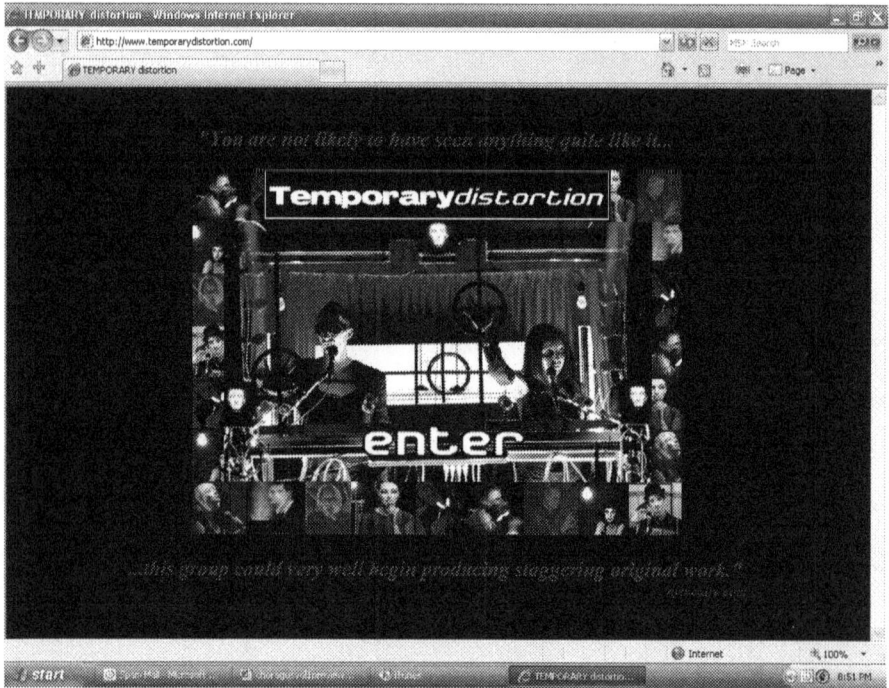

We've helped this very avant garde theatre group with some Web Hosting, Registration, and Rehearsal Space...no big deal. There very nice people. And here's a funny story about me and them, and our Funeral Home Offices:

Kenneth, Stacy and the gang were rehearsing one of their early weird performances (as opposed to their later weird performances) in a large, unused space just adjacent to our offices on the 4th Floor of the Thomas M. Quinn Memorial

Building, which happened to also be a large community Funeral Home.

It was late, 9 o'clock or so, and later in the year, so completely nighttime outside. I was tired and a bit burnt, and they were cheerily in their box, wearing their gasmasks and makeup, and playing their dirgelike music.

So, the doorman from the first floor comes up around 9 PM, to remind us that the building gets shut down a little after 9:30. OK, we say, we'll be done soon. We go back to our business.

20-30 minutes later, we make our way to the elevator. One of us presses the button, and nothing happens. Hmm. Well…maybe the thing is broken again. All of a sudden.

We take the stairs, and as we one-by-one get to the first floor, it becomes abundantly clear that the building is in the process of, or already has been shut down. Delightful.

We try the front door, which is quite clearly locked. All the lights are off, and there they are with their gasmasks and

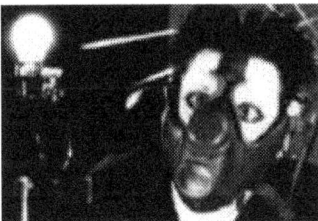

white face paint. In the Funeral Home. We all had places to go, so, after brief deliberation, we decided to just walk right out through the alarmed rear exit.

After about 5 seconds, we thought maybe the alarm hadn't been triggered. In 2 more seconds, we knew the truth. And boy was it loud.

So there we are, in the back of the Large Community Funeral Home. And, since we rushed to get out, the Temporary Distortion people, 5 or 6 of them, are still dressed all in black. Except for the white facepaint and the gas masks. And the mascara. And there I am, having just recently rented this very nice suite of offices that we probably can't afford.

Well, I've never been much for storytelling. So suffice it to say that no one got arrested or evicted. And both Happy Media and Temporary Distortion are, despite humble beginnings, still going strong.

***

(text from www.temporarydistortion.com)

Temporary *distortion* (T*d*) is a performance group led by writer, director, and designer Kenneth Collins that produces original works for the theatre. Unique nonlinear juxtapositions of text, image, and sound, these works have become increasingly focused on stillness, minimalism, and the search for a new style of chamber theatre performance—intimate and meditative.

Temporary *distortion* produces work that often asks to be seen from the perspective of a private hallucination or a dream...existing in a world where time seems to slow and meaning shifts. Focused on creating a delusionary and dreamlike stillness in its work, Temporary *distortion* seeks to counter the ever present frenetic rush found in popular media, New York City, and much other new theatre. Through its stillness, T*d*'s work explores a meditative quality that likens performance to poetry and makes room for association and reflection in the continuous present moment.

Entry Draft: Innovative Internships

Entry Draft is the Happy Media Network's exclusive apprenticeship and internship program. This program has been an unmatched opportunity for students from NYU, Fordham University, Columbia University, Baruch College, LaGuardia Community College, the NYC Board of Education's City-as-School Program, Washington University, and other educational institutions, as well as people from the community at large.

Entry Draft Interns can earn school credit, or just beef up their portfolios, by working on projects within the Happy Media Network. Right now we are seeking people with experience and interest in Media, Design, Computer Science, Finance, Economics, and Communications. This is an opportunity to acquire some well recognized experiential education in a comfortable and exciting working environment.

There are currently in-person and tele-internship opportunities in the fields of administration, design, branding/corporate identity, database creation and development, as well as in a number of more advanced technical fields. In-office locations include Astoria, NY, West New York, NJ, Litchfield, CT, and other locations.

Here is a partial roll call of the young people (not all of whom are still young) who have served time in our Entry Draft Program: Emmanuel, Nico, Mike, Kevin, Other Mike, Winnie Wong, Jeffrey, Albert, Helen, Gary, James, Chad, Jessica, other Jessica, Sherron, John, Sal, Keena, Greg, Mark, Melissa, Corey, Andy, Brandon, Opal, Joel, Kristin, LaToya, Grace, Rachel. Anna, Tristan, Jason, Other Other Mike, Maz, Eli, Jennifer, Roberto, Joseph, Ron, Ruben.

Our interns have gone on to make music, write for newspapers, become attorneys and other professionals, and serve their community and themselves in many ways. Here are a few of the benefits of an **Entry Draft** Internship:

- Improved Organization

- Self Motivation

- Management, Leadership, and Communication Skills

- Specialized Skill Competence

- Familiarity with SOP

What follows are a few examples of what they have to say about the program. These essays were written by students, as part of the City of New York's City-As-School Program.

The Entry Draft Internship Program is about experiential education. That is, about gaining experience in the task(s) one is looking to master. This means work. In healthy portions. And while our Mentors provide ample guidance and leadership, improvement of this kind happens when our interns begin to manage and motivate *themselves*. It's an unusual, and often remarkable process that simply can't be beat, when it comes to preparing people to function as active, competent professionals in their chosen field.

Internship Summary by Sarah

I am at the internship Happy Media. This is a web site designing company. It is one floor it has 2 rooms with 3 computers in each room and 2 other rooms (office) with desks and computers. My resource person Matt is here to guide me and help me learn what the company is about and how to design web sites. I am here to learn how to use the programs and design web pages (web sites) also to brush up on my computer skills.

The highlight of working at Happy Media was defiantly making my own web page, it was a lot of fun I had never done that before. While learning to use their programs what helped me the most was the web site www.fgcu.edu/support/office2000/frontpage it told me step by step what to do. It was very helpful it made it simple for beginners like me to understand.

My project is a web site with recipes that I had made at my previous internships along with a personal essay on how I came to the decision to go to culinary school and about my time being a pastry chef. It also has pictures of the pastries that I give recipes for and a few other pictures of my time as a pastry chef.

This like all my other internships has been really good experience for me and I was able to explore a job that I might have never had the chance to otherwise. I was also able to learn how to create web sites which may come in handy some day if I would like to make a web site on my own.

My project is a web site that has recipes, pictures, and an essay about my career as a pastry chef. The recipes are ones that I made at my last internship at Osteria del Circo. The pictures are of these deserts that I made.

To make the web site I used a program called Microsoft Front page. It was actually a lot easier than I thought it would be, all I had to do was make a page then choose a word that I wanted to be able to click on and connect to another page, so I would highlight the word then press control and "k" and then the pages would connect with that word. Then I played around with colors and font and then I added pictures and my essay, and there you have it a web page. It was simple as that, with a little extra like scanning the pictures etc.

When you open my page it say's "Sarah's bakery" and has a picture of me at a bakery I worked at with pastries. You then click on "Sarah's bakery" and it takes you to a table of contents you click on which place you want to go to. If you chose "From the beginning it takes you to my personal essay and if you click on the "Menu" it takes you to recipes. Once at the recipes you can choose which one you would like to view by clicking on it.

I learned a lot working here which will definitely come in handy in the future. You can access almost anything through the computer and when you know how to use it, it just makes life that much easier especially when I use the computer as much as I do.

Internship Summary by Gary

Happy Media is a new media developer and service provider. The nature of Happy Media is to provide goods and services to its costumers with 100% satisfaction guaranteed. Happy Media's philosophy is "to rid the world of evil, and provide superior, low-cost corporate, creative, internet and marketing services".

The person in charge of production is Matt. Matt's role at Happy Media or his position is director of operations. He's in charge of certain client's websites. He takes care of most of the technical and visuals applied to the corresponding websites.

My role as an intern here at Happy Media is to contribute my knowledge of computers and adapt them to the best of my ability to contribute to the success to this company. I offer my services like any other employee. I basically have been working on my own website project that I feel is very good. I named it BronxBmx.com or BxBmx.com for short. I think this site will launch a whole new understanding to life in the Bronx and how we ride and how we se things around us.

When I'm not glued to the computer working on my site, I'm helping out Matt with the countless emails that Happy Media receives every morning and giving suggestions to certain client's pages that need a little help. I also review text before it gets placed on the sight, not so much as spell check but more for the content of the text and what point there trying to get across.

As I mentioned, Creepy Crawly was the site that was given to us for our own input. We added links to the actual site. Links like Wal-Mart and Invisions. These links allow customers to purchase these items through our own provider. I also wrote text for the links. Smart, funny little remarks to make the customers interested in the products we're advertising for. We added backgrounds to the site. Anything from vampire bats images to skeleton head pictures to keep the amused. And also some effects, to give the site some life. Effects like flashing phrases and moaning sounds.

The reading project discusses how economics is the study of why people make one choice rather than another when buying and selling, spending and saving. It explains about goods and services. Goods being the product, and services being the person who distributes the product. It discusses about Scarcity, which means that there is not enough of everything to go around. That s the reason that we can't have everything we want.

Choices are a must in economics due to the fact that decisions must be made how best to use the natural resource, workers, and capital that are available. Choices also come with cost due to the fact that we don't have enough money to buy things we want at the same time. We might have to sacrifice one to get the other. It talks about the means of production to produce goods and services and how if the government owns and operates almost all of the nations means of production, then that nation's economic systems is called communism, for example, China. It also talks about the three different types of economic systems.

Capitalism, Socialism and Communism. Capitalism being a private ownership of means of production. Socialism, public and private ownership of means of productions. Communism, public ownership of means of production. An economic system is the way a group or nation organizes itself for production. The reading basically gave an overview of the economic structures that different societies live by and how they maintain and development through these various groups.

My creative project was my work on Creepy Crawly. Which I will be discussing as you read along. I'll talk about how it came about and what steps I took to get it to be were we last left off. This site won't be posted for a while due to the fact that it still requires some more fine-tuning.

This internship was a one in a lifetime experience for me because I never had a chance to ever work for a web provider like Happy Media. Happy Media help me expand mentally in ways to better myself for future jobs to meet the demands of the employers. I like working in this type of field because I like computers and I plan to go to school for computers so this internship kind of gave me a head start for that.

Internship Summary by Mark

Previously there was an overflow of Internet based companies, there were so many that some refer to it as the "dot com era". In recent times most of these companies have met with an untimely end due to poor management skills, unwise business decisions and lack of experience in the corporate world. Today most of these companies are gone and forgotten, however there are an elite few who have managed to thrive as their makeshift dot com brethren were ignominiously wiped out. Amongst the greatest of these elite few is **The Happy Media Network**.

I have had the privilege of completing my internship with and becoming a part of the family of The Happy Media Network. Happy Media is an Internet based company that designs web sites and provides many other web services including corporate identity packages, graphic design, market research, alternative promotion, content provision, traffic acceleration, corporate presentations, name creation, and turn-key solutions. The staff mainly consists of three interns (Mark, Winnie, Jeff), the Senior Developer (Emmanuel), the Head of Operations (Matthew) and the Executive Director (Adam). Outsourced servers, lawyers, publicists, writers, industry specific personnel, and numerous other members required to successfully operate a growing business also play very important roles within The Happy Media Network.

As a Happy Median novice my initial duties consisted solely of basic data entry. As time passed I was awarded the responsibility of greater and more meaningful tasks such as the creation of e-mail accounts, spam scanning, servicing clients via telephone, web surfing for information and many other tasks. A few of these tasks are newly developed skills; others are pre-attained abilities which were further developed by carrying out these assignments. I entered Happy Media as a fledgling intern, but due to my exemplary skill and outstanding performance I now proudly bear the title of *Media Design Specialist*. My main objective was to simply imbibe as much knowledge as I could, dealing with networking, computer systems and software. During my experience with Happy Media I was granted the opportunity to demonstrate my Java programming abilities. The program I constructed was more than sufficient and my supervisors were very pleased to discover another of my many hidden talents.

While at Happy Media I've realized that I would very much like to work permanently in an environment such as this one. I get along extremely well with my coworkers and my time, work and opinion are greatly appreciated. My internship experience has enhanced my personal career direction. I have always known that I wanted to work with computers and in a world seamlessly controlled and driven by digital technology it was simply inevitable. As I pursue my career in the computer field the skills, abilities and knowledge I have gained will enable me to efficiently carry out many tasks demanded of me in future occupational endeavors. I still plan to eventually transfer to a senior college, however in the mean time I would love to work permanently in an atmosphere similar to the one at Happy Media, if not Happy Media itself. As I stated earlier I was given the opportunity to use my programming skills, skills that I acquired in school and developed on my own. I was given the task of creating a program that allowed the user to search a database and view results from that search by entering a personal identification number. My supervisors were more than pleased with the outcome.

I like everything about my internship. I was pleased with the expertise of my coworkers. Everyone possessed different skills and capabilities, so there was always something new to learn or teach. The workload was just right, enough to keep you interested and get you to understand what you're doing, but not so much that you get sick of it. I also loved the fact that I didn't have to wear a suit and tie every day. I would definitely recommend this experience to other students. It is a wonderful learning opportunity if you're interested in the field of computers.

The only minor detail I can think of that would improve this internship experience would be getting $ PAID $ for it. Traveling back and forth to school and work really had a severe impact on my dwindling bank account. Getting paid to absorb all you can at The Happy Media Network would be synonymous with "having your cake and eating it too". The only thing that would have made this internship a better learning experience for me would be the privilege of bringing most of the software home so I could spend more time learning how to use them properly, efficiently, and thoroughly. Overall, my position at Happy Media as a Media Design Specialist is quite possibly the greatest utilization of my time and money.

Internship Summary by Anthony

My name is Anthony and my summer school internship took place at the company Happy Media. Happy Media is a company that creates websites. Some of the websites that they have created have been for major corporations, and up & coming artists.

In my opinion Happy Media was one of the best resources I've had thus far. The work wasn't overwhelming and they treated us like adults. I've had many, longer, internships and I enjoyed the short time at Happy Media. I wouldn't of changed the experience, because we still got things done but not in a pressure filled environment. Overall I learned a lot about making websites at Happy Media, because my project was to make my own. It was actually interesting and it's a way to channel my creativity. Before coming to Happy Media I had no particular interest in computers, but now I know it's more than typing and other tedious activities.

On a daily basis at Happy Media I basically visited the Happy Media website and looked for non-working sites and links. Also I was looking for spelling, coding, and any other errors. In addition to using the computer I also kept the desks clean and threw out garbage and organized files, software, and hardware. It was pretty much standard office work.

As a whole the time spent at Happy Media was a successful experience. In addition to learning new computer skills, I also worked well with the rest of the interns. It was a meaningful experience, especially since it's my last internship at City-As-School.

Internship Summary by Kaysone

My name is Kaysone, and I was an intern at Happy Media. Happy Media is a place where Corporations and businesses go to for their websites to be fixed and updated; The Company was founded in 1997. My resource currently has 3 people working full-time with many interns working with them.

My resource person(s) is Matt LaRose and Adam Sherwin. Adam is the Executive Director of Operations, he helps with day-to-day promotions, overseeing and managing the offices. Matt directs all of the interns and he is the Director of Operations. He maintains and updates corporation and client's websites.

My part in this resource is to help with the updating and organizing of websites that Happy Media is currently working on. Further I helped with the organization with E-mail accounts on the website Good Homes.com. I directed and fixed where and how to contact certain brokers through out the United States.

The project I will be working on is about me and Eva Pigford America's next top model, I picked the topic on me and Eva cause I know who I am and I love Eva she is one of my idols. I learned how 2 use the computer and type faster, however I didn't know how to use the computer and type as fast as I can now, further I also learned how leading design programs such as MS FrontPage and Adobe Photoshop, which I didn't even knew existed until I came to Happy Media. When I came into this internship site it looked boring probably because of what some of the people were saying about computers. But now from this experience I can operate and maintain and even use computers as well as some professional web casters can do.

Welcome to my Internship by unknown

Hey wats up thanx 4 cumin thru N viewin mah page.

Da reason y im doin dis webpage is 4 a class project th@ I was asign 2 do.

Im doin dis page @ a resource/internship named <u>Happy Media</u> Where dey create their own web pages 4 many different companies.

Ive bin @ this resource for about 2 weeks, and wat i do here is well basically b online all day until i leave. Nah, but so far wat ive done here is check da many websites they have partnerships with and see if the website went through. If it didnt i had to copy and paste da name of it and the URL to a notepad program where one of the empolyers wood cum and check it to fix da problem.

Im doing this internship 4 credits th@ i have to accumalate so th@ i can finsh high skool.

@ mah skool CITY~AS~SKOOL, we get the opportunity not only to pick a resource/internship th@ we want but we also have da oportunity 2 pick wat classes we want 2 b in. Instead of being in a set class like regular high skools students have 2.

.:^:.Otha Internships Ive Bin In.:^:.

@ City~As. I had the opportunity to be in many different resources such as.

The Cobble Hill Health Center: Where I transported the residents that lived @ the nursing home to and from therapy.

The Animal Medical Center: Where i was an assistant to the veternarian technician. I helped in holding the animals while the technician would inject the animal with needles. I also had to clean out the many diferent wards/departments th@ the Medical center had.

The Astoria Performing Arts Center

As I write this (09/16/06), APAC is getting ready to celebrate its 5th Birthday. Happy Media is proud to have been working with the Astoria Performing Arts Center for a large portion of that time. I'm lucky enough to serve on their Board of Directors, as Executive Director Taryn Drongowski and Creative Director Brian Swasey shepherd the organization towards its own 10th Birthday. The text below is from the APAC website.

The Astoria Performing Arts Center (APAC) is dedicated to providing high quality theatre and entertainment at an affordable cost for the Astoria/LIC communities and to supporting local youth. APAC is a not-for-profit arts organization that couples professional theatre programming with community outreach efforts.

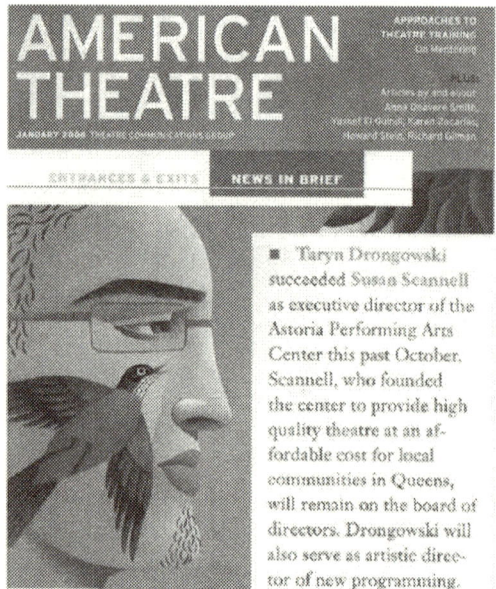

AMERICAN THEATRE

APPROACHES TO THEATRE TRAINING

ENTRANCES & EXITS   NEWS IN BRIEF

■ Taryn Drongowski succeeded Susan Scannell as executive director of the Astoria Performing Arts Center this past October. Scannell, who founded the center to provide high quality theatre at an affordable cost for local communities in Queens, will remain on the board of directors. Drongowski will also serve as artistic director of new programming.

Each year, APAC brings extended networks of artists, technicians and interns together to produce major musicals, classical, and modern plays. Examples from its youth and senior programming portfolio include an annual free summer intensive musical theatre training program for Astoria's 4rd –8th

graders ("Summer Stars"), and bringing live entertainment to various senior centers in Astoria. APAC strives to create innovative and engaging work equaling that of the most established and accomplished off Broadway New York theatre companies.

The work APAC produces is accessible, in a broad sense: the programming is varied in order to cultivate a broad audience, produced regularly each season, and affordable –so that theater-going can become a habit--not just a rare treat.

A New Home

With funding from the New York Department of Cultural Affairs (for which we have APAC supporter Peter Vallone Jr to thank!), APAC will be seeking a permanent home in Astoria/LIC.

From its beginning, the Astoria Performing Arts Center has been blessed with support from, literally, thousands—volunteers, actors, technicians, government officials, Astoria business owners, the press, teachers, and many, many others. We strive to earn and repay that support by producing shows of the highest quality and by seeking out opportunities to give back to the community.

The Greater Astoria Historical Society

Happy Media's Director of Operations, Matt LaRose, is lucky enough to serve on the Board of Directors of the GAHS. This fine organization still resides at 3520 Broadway in Astoria, where Happy Media had it's suite of offices.

The Greater Astoria Historical Society, chartered in 1985, is a non-profit cultural and community oriented organization dedicated to preserving the past and promoting Long Island City's future. The Society hosts field trips, walking tours, slide presentations, and guest lectures for schools and the public.

"History is the most powerful tool that a society processes. It tells us why the things we value are the things we should value, and it tells us the things that should be ignored. That is true power, a profound power -- the power to define a whole society."   Text from astorialic.org

Corporate Naming

A brand name for a Company, Venture, Product, Service, or Project should be easy to say, spell and remember, for starters. It should also be evocative, powerful, and free of negative connotations or potential Intellectual Property conflicts. It should extol the benefits of the product.

Ultimately, this is the area in which Happy Media has excelled more than any other, in these first 10 years. We've created more than 250 top-quality Corporate Names for our Network, in nearly every category imaginable. We've also been lucky enough to come up with a proven-effective system for creating more, either for clients (do call us today!) or for additional Happy Media owned properties.

We know that our Corporate Names are of the highest quality for several reasons. Those that coming immediately to mind are:

1. They are all easy to say, spell, and remember

2. They are all evocative, powerful, free of negative connotations, or potential Intellectual Property conflicts.

3. They extol the benefits of the product, as all effective advertising should.

4. Professional people are always telling us, "Hey, that's a great name!"

5. We've sold more than two dozen of them, with an average sale price in the mid 4 figures.

6. We have a background in writing, editing, branding, marketing, research, and promotion that gives a very good idea of what will generate a desired reaction, in a desired demographic.

Happy Media has been building brands online since 1997. Corporate Naming is not something to be taken lightly. Even after creating more than 250, I still have the passion for this area of work.

From the beginning, we've been focused, IP speaking, on our ability to use a particular name, not on preventing others from doing so. For example, on the tv right now, sometimes both at once, are two shows called Weekly Update and Tech Toys. Now, we've been using these two brand names since the late 90s. They've been a steady part of what we do. So it won't surprise us in the least when we see that those shows are no longer around in 6 months or a year, while our Weekly Update (newsletter) and Tech Toys (consumer electronics) just keeps on grinding away.

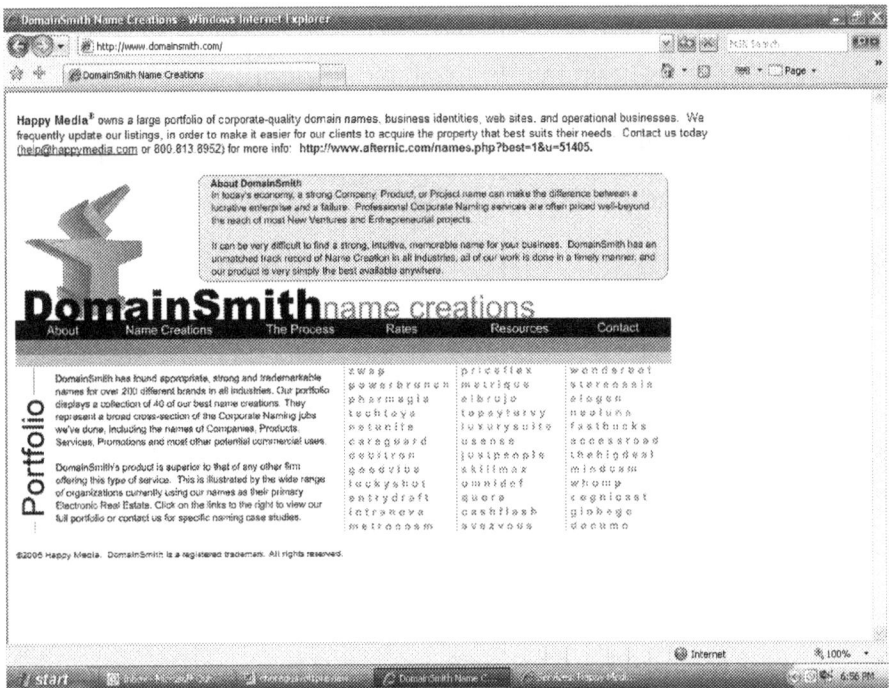

We're not looking for clients these days in internet services or graphic design, or other aspects of corporate identity work. We are always, however, looking for corporate naming work. And, all kidding aside…I'm pretty damn good all by myself, but when we get the whole Network abuzz about a project, we really can't be beat.

eBusiness

Cybermarketing

A rose by any other name...

Domain names are selling for up to $1 million a letter. While some may be worth it, even seasoned executives are confusing a great URL with a great business plan, according to the experts.

by Dave Webb, eBusiness Journal, November 2000

The Web site of branding consultants Burson Marsteller quotes Cervantes' legendary Don Quixote: "A good name is better than riches."

It must be so. Online businesses are still trading their riches for good domain names. And the attitude still seems to be the more generic, the better.

Is the watershed of the domain speculation industry the $3-million-plus (US) purchase by search engine company AltaVista of www.altavista.com from a similarly named software developer? No. It's the $7.5-million sale of business.com a year ago to eCompanies LLP, which plans to turn the domain into the portal for small business. Seller Marc Ostrofsky had bought the domain name for a then-staggering $150,000 in 1996.

"Right now, a good domain name goes for $1 million a letter," says Naseem Javed, founder of Brampton, Ont.-based ABC Namebank International.

Javed was a pioneer when he focused on the corporate naming business 22 years ago. While advertising agencies and marketing companies often came up with company names as part of a larger campaign, ABC Namebank was one of the first companies to specialize exclusively in the name game.

Domain and dot-com company names can be valuable assets. But most of the time, they're not, Javed says.

"Ninety per cent of corporate names are in the process of chipping away at company assets," he says.

Why the nominal crisis?

"There's a general misconception that we are all out of names, that we're only left with zodiac signs, major rivers and reptiles," he says.

"There is no shortage of names."

The problem is that people naming companies have no formal training and precious little experience on the naming front. They're left to focus groups, lists of suggestions from groups of employees, and blind guessing. And that's led to billions of dollars' worth of brand maneuvering around those names.

"Amateurs have no place in naming today. Those days are over," he says.

Generics — like business.com — are an attractive alternative to a branding campaign that makes $1 million a letter look like petty cash, says Javed.

But how effective will such names be when the majority of users aren't new to the Web and have more sophisticated keyword capabilities and experience using them?

"Fast-forward five years," says Adam Sherwin, executive director of New York-based Happy Media Inc.

"Take away the dot-com, and you have no brand. Even Business Etc. would have a better chance.

"A memorable, powerful, intuitive, creative brand name will always have the advantage over a generic equivalent."

More to the point, though, is that even seasoned executives can believe a great domain name is a substitute for a business plan or a revenue model. Sometimes, that seven-figure domain name comprises most of a company's assets, and is often "the only thing like an idea they've got."

"A Web site does not a company make, and it certainly does not a viable business make."

Generics can be valuable, says Sherwin, especially to the online presences of brick-and-mortar retailers.

"For example, WalMart could attract a significant number of clients to its online pharmacy store by setting up a domain name such as flu.com," he says.

(Flu.com is one of almost 100 generic domain names Procter & Gamble has amassed over the years, and is selling through GreatDomains.com. Among the others: beautiful.com, cleans.com, sensual.com, romantic.com, scent.com and thirst.com.)

But a Web-based company has different needs for its domain name, says Sherwin. Take, for example, Happy Media itself.

Founded in 1996, Happy Media operated out of Sherwin's living room until earlier this year. Customers don't stumble across Happy Media in the street, or pop by the office — they contact the company over the Web.

But the company has developed a network of services, each of which requires its own touch point to avoid alienating customers.

Happy Media handles small business and individual branding and naming clients through its DomainSmith brand. Its GreatServers brand is aimed at the high-end hosting market. If a client comes to Happy Media for the former and gets the latter, she's not going to want to do business.

"These two brands represent closely related parts of the same process, but by branding them individually, the company can access customers in an efficient, targeted fashion," he says.

The corporate and online identities are "two sides of the coin," Javed says, and a clever domain name that can't be fully leveraged is worthless. "Without the trademark, you have nothing," says Javed. What's left of cocacola.com or sony.com without the brand power of the corporate identity?

"All you're left with is metal or sugar and junk of no value," he says.

And, of course, Javed has words for boo.com, the dot-com retailer that burned through $130 million (US) in six months before closing its doors: "Take a look at your stupid name. What were you trying to achieve?"

He slots boo.com among the Yahoo!-inspired trend of "moronic names."

"Sugar-coated branding tricks," he dismisses them. "They never work."

Wicked Slice

Oddly enough, for someone who has the bug so damn bad…I'm pretty good. I've played just a few more than 100 rounds, over the course of two full seasons. By the end of the first season, I was regularly shooting in the mid-90s on a bunch of different courses.

At the end of that season, I had surgery on a Torn Posterior Labrum in my right shoulder, followed by 6 months of physical therapy. By the end of this, my second season (10/24/06), I'm regularly shooting in the 80s, and my handicap has dropped to 16.6.

For the record, I rarely slice. I do have a natural, ahem, fade, but I can work the ball right to left if I need to. Sure, the Big Right Ball is a problem of mine from time to time. But it doesn't happen too often. And when it does, it's really much more of a block than a wicked slice.

Happy Media's golf web sites, Wicked Slice (for casual players) and Golf Clan (for people with golf dreams), provide original, informative Golf Course Profiles, the latest Offbeat Golf News, cool Wicked Slice Designs, and top brand gear and accessories. We're committed to bringing you top-notch Golf Lifestyle Publications. And we sure do love the game of golf.

If you represent a golf course who'd like to have a clear, professional, marketable profile written about your course, drop me a line anytime. What follows are a few of these profiles, included among a selection of the golf writing I've managed to squeeze into my schedule in the two years since that first swing. Some Course Profiles, some swing thoughts, and one overwrought imagining of what it will, yes will, be like to shoot 70 on my home course.

The Right Attitude

I have never, to my knowledge, been accused of having the right attitude. And yet, about this one thing, this simple, elegant game that sends accountants and judges to the tossing of clubs, I can honestly say that I've got the right idea. When I mis-swing (which is often enough, given my newness to the sport), all I do, all I can do, is giggle my ass off.

Business and Golf

As many of you already know, I've only recently taken up the game. I got my first set of golf clubs (from my wife Amey) for my 29th Birthday, a few months after our wedding. Not wanting to embarrass myself too badly on the course, I spent that Winter (or, more accurately, Mid-September until Late January) sweating at the driving range. Once I felt comfortable enough, I prepared to play.

My chance came on January 26, at the Key West Golf Club. When we arrived in town, I made myself an early morning tee-time, so as to best protect my here-to-fore untested game from the judging eyes of the golfing public. I hit a few balls in the small cage-like range at the attractive club, and in the dewy early morning light, I teed it up.

Almost instantly, productivity here at HM Headquarters decreased dramatically. Just kidding. In reality, a golf course is one of the few traditional networking environments in which I'm willing to spend any time. Since January of 2005, I've played roughly 100 rounds at 30+ courses in 8 states and Canada. I've played with all sorts of people I didn't know beforehand, including Bartenders, a Private Investigator, a Carpenter, Investment Bankers, Sanitation Workers, Students, Bartenders, Judges, Lawyers, and Students. And boy, am I feeling more positive than usual about people, and about the work I do. Drop me a line anytime if you'd like to play.

In both business and golf, I feel that one can increase one's likelihood of success by sticking to few essential principles. For example, in business, it's an essential principle that you must generate more revenue than you spend. As such, diversifying your sustainable revenue streams is the paramount goal. And in golf, an essential principle is that you must hit your ball into the hole in as few strokes as possible. As such, maintaining control of your ball is the paramount goal.

Key West Golf Club

The southernmost golf course in the continental U.S. is, despite the $150+ price tag, an excellent choice for golfers of any skill level. It's a good quality course with a low-key, uncrowded atmosphere, and a very friendly staff.

Located at the entrance to the island of Key West, the 18-hole 200 acre Key West Golf Club was designed by Rees Jones, and features stately palms, dense mangrove lined fairways, serene lakes, and undulating multi-tiered greens. This public course measures 6,500 from the tips and 3 sets of tees will challenge players of all abilities. This course is the southern most golfing facility in the continental U.S. Since 1994, the course has been brought up to a championship-quality level. All of the fairways and bunkers have been refurbished, in order to give golfers a better conditioned facility.

At the entrance to the island of Key West, the unique Key West Golf Club's 18 holes encompass over 200 acres of beautiful Florida Keys foliage and wildlife. Stately palms ... dense mangroves... serene lakes... rolling fairways and dramatic greens... egrets in the distance... clean, clear tradewinds...

Golf legend REES JONES masterfully designed this public, 18 hole, 6,500 yard course to be a challenge to players of all abilities. Come meet all the exciting challenges of the course, including the infamous "Mangrove Hole" (143 yards, par 3 that is played completely over a field of thickly intertwined tropical mangroves).

Putting

I feel strongly that keeping quiet arms, hands, and wrists, and letting the shoulders and back move the clubhead, is the way to go. That said, putting a golf ball, even putting it well, can be perhaps to most unathletic endeavor imaginable... and still work just fine if the nerves are in check.

Speed is, I think, the second key issue. In most cases, the line of a putt is going to be fairly readable. Which means that if one's speed is right, the worst case scenario is a tap in. A sure 2 putt is a sure way to play to one's potential, and avoid the dreaded Big Number.

Grinding out Pars

I've been playing this game for less than two years. There's one month left in my second season. I've played just over 100 rounds, with Major Shoulder Surgery around Round 60. And I can honestly tell you that there are stretches of rounds, whole sides sometimes, where I'm confident of grinding my way to 4 or 5 pars over a stretch of holes.

Driving the Ball

The reasons it should be a strength to any serious player are many. Two essentials will suffice:

1. It starts off the hole

2. There's not much to it.

Unlike many iron shots, and the short game, most of the time golfers are given the opportunity to just give it a whack, with no too-much attention given to nuance and creativity. Line up the clubhead, line up the shoulders, line up the feet, back and through.

9.24.06

Well, since the 20th, I've officially achieved my original goal for this 2nd golf season. With 1 full month to spare. When I started out chipping again this March, after 1 season of play (about 60 rounds) and Major Shoulder Surgery (Oct. 5th), I felt that I had a good chance to get my handicap at or below 18 before the Official end of season here in CT, November 1.

I'm at 17.4 now, 40 or so rounds later. I haven't been playing particularly well or often the last few weeks, but the next four days, Monday through Thursday, look like good weather for multiple round days.

9.25.06

Honestly felt, for not the first, time, like I was using someone else's hands today. Usually I'm a reasonably good ball-striker; my misses are usually not as bad as could be. But today, I couldn't even seem to lay up properly…and most of the times that I felt I'd made a good swing, I came up or down a hill to find out that I'd landed just short. Or rolled off just slightly long.

The Samoset

I recently returned from a delightful, much-needed vacation. My wife and I took a 12-day odyssey throughout New

England. During the trip I turned 30, Summer Ended, and I played 7 rounds of golf in 12 days at 5 different courses in 4 State/Provinces in 2 countries.

We went from NYC to Great Barrington, MA, to Hillsboro, NH, to Rockport, ME, to Quebec City, QE to South Royalton, VT, to Windsor, CT to New Haven, CT, then finally home.

It was a lot of fun, remarkably relaxing (given the frenetic pace), and I intend to do a great deal of writing about it in this space over the next six months. Which brings me to my next point...I'm having arthroscopic shoulder surgery next week, which will give you and I much more time together, as I heal and rehabilitate the joint and the rest of me. My father is also having much more serious surgery a week later, which should make us very fun people to be around as The Holidays speed towards us.

Lido Golf Club

If you're looking for a gem of a Robert Trent Jones Sr. designed course, just minutes from Brooklyn, Queens, and Manhattan...most folks would assume that you're out of luck. Not so, thanks to Lido Golf Club. An historic, oft-imitated classic that has recently undergone yet another renaissance.

The Facility

When you first arrive down south of the Meadowbrook Parkway, near Point Lookout and Long Beach, you'll notice a very pleasant atmosphere. Friendly but not too overbearing…just enough to let you know you're welcome, but not so much that you feel like you're at a theme park.

At our early arrival of 7:30 there were not yet balls in the machine at the range. But we found a nice empty golf course, attentive enough staff, and a facility that's put together well enough that you're ready to get started right away. Pro shop, café, practice areas (irons only range and 2 putting greens, one of which allows chipping) are all central located and easy to use. They also have extensive resources for corporate outings and other events, and nice touches like plentiful course stations, an outdoor bar/barbeque for the busy season, and a very professional, well put-together scorecard and yardage book.

The Course

Plenty of wind and water, but a well put together, and cared-for, golf course. No carts due to the wet, but again…it was uncrowded and the pull carts were right there for the taking. When it gets crowded, as the staff told me it definitely does (this place is very close to NYC and JFK in particular) one would need to ride in order to enjoy the experience, which is not unusual.

The Sixteenth is an amazing bit of risk-reward artistry. It's a vicious par-5 that has not one, but two forced carries over Reynolds Channel. For the original, the PGA's only site says "Many golf course aficionados today speak of links-style Lido Golf Club in the same reverent tones scientists and archeologists talk about the ancient library at Alexandria -- an invaluable treasure whose loss was a blow for all mankind."

The 6 holes that run along the channel are more than a little seductive. Much of the middle of the course is a bit confusing for a first time player, with many holes running together. And boy...is this course long. But even for this novice golfer, Lido is a track well worth revisiting again and again.

Stonybrook Golf

One of the most challenging nine hole courses in Connecticut, Stonybrook GC is located in Litchfield, Connecticut. The Stonybrook pro shop offers a wide range of golf equipment and apparel. After you finish a memorable round of golf, enjoy food and drink at the grill. Remember to reserve a tee time for your next visit. The friendly, attentive staff will be happy to call and a secure a reservation for you.

70 at my home course

Every hole I'm about to describe, every shot, that is, has happened already. Like most golfers, just not all in the same round. I've just started playing this game, however, so I'm still cautiously optimistic that my day will come.

1st Hole

I start off on the 535-yard Par 5 1st. Within view of the clubhouse, I lay my usual cut down the right side of the ample fairway. This opens up the second shot for a halfway sculled (nerves) hybrid 3-iron, which stays low, but winds up more or less where I wanted. I've got 133 to the center of the green, with trees hard left, and a steep slope on the right side of the elevated green.

As usual, I don't quite bring my 8-iron in right-to-left enough, and my approach bounces hard right off the right side of the hump, down to the bottom of the swale near the tree and dirt cart path. However, I've had this chip before, and I knock it up and over to within 4 feet, then hit the par putt.

2nd Hole

I get ahold of my usual little skank cut, which leaves me 170 downhill to the center of the tiny green at this 384-yard Par 4. I thin a five iron to the front of the green-guarding bunkers. I chip over them, but leave myself 12 feet for par. No go...I tap in for bogey.

3rd Hole

This Par 3 is almost always a 7-iron for me. Today it plays 145 into the wind. I pull it a bit, but it lands hard left of the green, and the slope brings it back onto the left side of the green.   Downhill 12 feet…two putts. Par.

4th Hole

This tee shot requires a slight draw to set up the best angle to the dogleg left green. I rarely hit a draw, except on this hole. For once, I nail it, leaving myself in the center of the sloping fairway, 119 to the center of the green. I underclub a bit with a 9 iron, but hit it just right, leaving myself with a slightly downhill, left-to-right 4-footer for birdy. To get myself back to par. I give it pretty good speed…but don't get it high enough. I make the 2 footer for par.

5th Hole

My drive down the right side is long enough to clear the trees on the left, but doesn't take its usual kick to the left, and runs into the rough. I've got…ugly. The ball is above my feet and sidehill, and what I need to do is get the ball up, and keep it there, but still have it land softly. I've got 155 with a stream, a very elevated (40 feet), narrow, rolling green. Guarded directly by a deep potbunker. There is a steep slope behind the green, and anything hit off of it is likely to keep going back down the hill.

Normally a 7-iron is my 150-yard club, but it would seem to be out of the question, given the lie. A five would work, but I don't think it would keep the ball airborne enough to get up the hill. I settle on a six, and give it a whack.

I get it up there, but a little left and a little short. I've got a 15-foot, uphill then down a sidehill chip to a pin halfway up a slope. With the 60-degree, I put my weight on the left side, then, just like in the backyard, I slip the club under the ball and pop it goes. Just over the hole, but the slope carries it down a bit.

I've got a downhill breaking 1 ½ footer for par, and it lips out. Bogey. I'm two over after five holes.

6th Hole

I lick my chops every time I make the hike or ride up the steep hill above the 5th green. This hole is the best birdie opportunity of the par 4s on this course. I take driver, and the idea is to fade the ball just to the right of a small tree at about the 230 mark. I leave it a bit left of the tree, and I've got a 65 yard downhill pitch, but to a very receptive green. Ideally, one would keep the pitch high and right, and let the slope of the green carry the ball over towards the pin. I hit the shot, if a bit chunky, and I find myself four feet below the hole, putting for birdie. I must have nerves already because I stub the put, and it doesn't get there. I tap in for par.

7th Hole

I drive the ball straight downhill, to the edge of the stream running across the hole at the end of the fairway. From there, it's a fairly stock 8 iron to the front edge of the two-tiered green. Two putts…par.

8th Hole

Another uneventful hole. I over cooked my drive a bit, and left it farther left on the fairway than usual. But that's actually a cleaner angle into the well-bunkered green. Two putts...par.

9th Hole

For me, this is the toughest hole on the course. 160 something yards, perched at least 25 up a steep hill on the side of the clubhouse. I usually overclub a bit, in this case, feeling a bit strong, I grab a 5-iron. Not unusually, I leave it too far to the right, and when it's done rolling down the hill, it's pretty damn close the bench at Tee 3.

I've had this shot before...dozens of times. But it converts into a bogie, IF I make this 60 yard uphill pitch just right. The green slopes very downhill away from where I'll have any chance of getting it up and on. I choose a 52-degree Gap Wedge, in the hopes that the slope the ball is on will give it enough loft.

I get all my weight forward, and take a few slow swipes. Feels just about right. I'll need to land it just in the fringe at the top of the green, and hopefully that will deaden it enough to have just trickle, not race, down the hill towards the hole and the almost inevitable run off of the green altogether.

I step to the ball…and bring the club back, and just then, the loud screen door of the clubhouse deck, which overlooks this green, SLAMS back into its housing.

It's rare for me stop a swing, once I get started. And I'm very rarely spooked by loud noises on the course. I'm also, however, never just 2 over after 8 holes.

My head snaps up just a mite, and I pull off the ball just a hair. Instead of the very top edge of the green, for which I was aiming, the ball heads left, low, hard. It hits the slope once, then again at the very top, and lands, softly as if lightly tossed, three yards off the side of the green…and 4 yards below the cup.

I quickly, somewhat calmly, head up the hill, lay my wedge by the stick as I lay it out, take a deep breath and practice stroke, and stiffly easy as can be, stroke the putt into the dead center of the hole.

The Turn

Now my home course is a 9-holer. It's very well maintained, and you really have to hit your spots, but it's still a short 9-holer. So, for the purpose of this back 9, we'll be playing the same 9 holes, but from the tips, extending the course to its full just over 6,000 yard form.

10th Hole

I start off on the 535-yard Par 5 1st. I try to lay my usual cut down the right side of the ample fairway, but come out of it a bit, and leave it hard right, in the rough but clear of any trees. My 3-iron is better this time, albeit from farther back.

I've got 148 to the center, and my approach bounces twice on the front of the green and stops dead, hole high. 6 footer straight in until the end, when it falls off. I tap in for par.

11th Hole

Instead of my usual little skank cut, I overcook this one, and find myself back behind a tree in the left rough. I play a 6 iron nicely out to just right of the green. Hoping to get the ball just below the hole, I chip with my 56-degree sand wedge. It goes up and around the sloped green, and for just a moment I think it's going to slide in the hole (it's done it before), but it heads right on by, and checks up about 18 inches past. A near perfect lag put. I hit the comebacker for par. Still two over.

12th Hole

This Par 3 is almost always a 7-iron for me, from any tee. From this tee, all the way down the hill, it plays 150 into the wind, and a little bit uphill. The pin is on the lower part of a heavily sloped (back from front, and left to right) green. I still pull the 7-iron. I hit it pretty well, but leave it a bit short, 12 or 15 feet below the hole, just off the fringe in the mid rough, slightly buried.

Now, I don't make that many birdies. I've birdied every hole on this course, but this here par 3, and the par 4 sixth, are certainly my best chances for birdie. So I really need to, if not make this, then be sure of the next, and hope for the best.

Lob Wedge or 56-degree? Hard downward chop, or smooth, solid bump? I'm in the mid-rough, but the ball is sitting up just a bit. I decide on a nice, extended pendulum putting stroke with the 56-degree, which should run up the slope pretty well if I hit it. I've got to be firm with this one to get it up the hill. But I don't, under any circumstances, want to run it by the hole, leaving myself the dreaded downhill comebacker.

I've made plenty of pars from down here before. And 1 birdie that I can think of...but also a few double bogies.

I give it a good run, and the speed looks right, but it's left all the way. When suddenly just a foot or so short of the hole, the ball takes a wicked hop to the right, and rolls right in the cup. Birdie 2, and I'm 1 over after 12 holes, by far the best start I've had. Ever.

13th Hole

This 376 Yard par four requires a fairly hard draw off the tee to avoid rolling off the heavily sloped right side into or just beyond a stand of trees separating the hole from the 6th.

Not unusually, I block it right. The Big Right Ball that plagues me, and so many others, under times of stress. I really get this one good, and it heads hard right towards the trees that line that side. I wind up pretty much out of play. My patented 5-iron chip back into the fairway gets me out of trouble, but any cushion I might have on this hole, and for this round, is gone.

I've got 122 to the center of the green. A mellow 8 for me, on this hole, on a normal day. But now my nerves are a bit jangled. These are the times when I could really use a rubber band, to keep around my wrist. I'd snap it, to get myself focused again. I've tried a few, but haven't found one yet that was thick enough to inflict a little pain, but still fit around my wrist. Anyway…I knock it to within 5 feet, and hit the putt. Par. I'm still just 1 over.

14th Hole

My drive down the right side is, once again, long enough to clear the trees on the left, but this time it takes its usual kick to the left. I've got 125 to the center of the green. Another eight iron. I narrowly miss the birdie putt, and tap in for par.

15th Hole

Here it is. Of the remaining 4 holes, this one, a 330-yard Par 4, is by far my best chance for a birdie. The blue tee for this hole is halfway up the hill, leaving a blind, uphill chute of a drive. Need to keep this one left enough to get a good look at the green.

My drive goes up and over the slope of the fairway…a real shot by my standards. Easily 280. Too much of a shot, as it turns out. I run out of fairway, and find myself on the steep slope about 60 yards above the green. An awkward pitch, to say the least.

I pull out the 56-degree wedge, then choose the 52 degree instead, wanting to make sure that I get good, solid contact, and don't either

a) Blade the shot over the top of the green, sending it down the perilously steep other side, 60 yards down onto the 16th Tee.

b) Chunk it short, into the deep grass bunker guarding the right side from where I am now perched.

Good choice. I give it a good dead-wristed thump, and it goes up and splat against the tilted green, then drifts lazily towards the whole, winding up about 6 feet below the hole.

I tend to have speed control issues. This is my best remaining chance, by far, to even have a birdie putt. So I really can't leave this one short of the hole.

I don't leave it short, but I do leave it a few inches left. I tap in for par.

16th Hole

Taking it straight downhill again, I get it stuck a little bit behind the ball. I'm left, on the edge of the stream running the left side of the hole. I've got 165 up the hill, to a heavily sloped, two tier green. Can't be long here or right, and short or left isn't great either. And I really need to take enough club.

This shot should play to about 185, and a fairly noticeable breeze has picked up. I'd try to sting an old-fashioned three-iron bouncebounce up the hill, but I can't be sure that that shot will get across the stream before it does its bouncebounce routine.

I choose a hybrid 4-iron. Hoping that the added loft will keep it up. I'll just have to hit it well enough to get up there, even if it's on one hop.

I get it solid, and it leaves me on the edge of the green. The pin is up, however, so that's only about 8 feet short of the hole. Two putts, par.

17th Hole

Well, it's been a hell of a round. I'm 1 little stroke over par with 2 to play, and I'm feeling pretty good. The pressure of trying to shoot par is pretty much over, so I swing pretty freely, and lace a line shot to the edge of the stream. A ¾ pitching wedge to within 12 feet. Two putts, par.

18th Hole

The tee is a t the very tip of the box on this last hole, nearly in the road. What might have been 160 yards up the hill is now about 190, playing well over 210. I pull my hybrid 3-iron out of the bag, and give it a waggle. I need to keep this ball left of the green, if I don't get it up on there.

Still loose, I knock it stiff, left of the hole but too many bounces. I've left myself 15 feet above the hole, with the first 8 feet being rolling rough, and the next 7 feet being hard left-to-right downhill.

And just then, a funny thing happened. I reached into my bag for my 60-degree wedge and my putter, and suddenly, clear as day, I saw the chip in my mind. I saw the clubface fanned open, sliding under the ball and then…click. I saw the ball take two hops, one in the rough and one in the fringe well left and above the hole, and slowly start to trickle down the hill.

I smiled. Looked above me to make sure someone was watching, from the balcony above. I dropped my putter back into the bag, grabbing just the 56-degree. I took a couple of light, airy mock-chips, and then gripped and set the clubhead behind the ball. I set my feet up open and weighted my left side. And…visit www.wickedslice.com to find out what happened, and get a free Golf Visor.

State of the Web

I think that this would be a good time to address an unfortunate, but ultimately minor, issue with regards to the Happy Media Network. We own and operate more than 250 internet properties. We most enjoy providing original web content, content aggregation, and affiliate links for your surfing pleasure (see Daily Examiner, Wicked Slice, Lucky Shot, et al). However, the revenue generated by these types of sites tends to be rather less than a little. And so, periodically according to finances, Happy Media is forced to take our otherwise quite original and entertaining web sites (see Good Homes, Whomp, Topsy Turvy, et al), and temporarily point them towards Paid Parking Programs that lack original content.

As I write this (12/16), about a month after the previous paragraph, things have changed just a bit for the better, with regards to our Paid Parking Provider. Our options for customizing the landing page for any and all parked domains have grown significantly. We're able to manipulate and upload images, text, formatting, and pretty much everything that makes a web site unique. We're excited about this. And I personally have been up quite late the last few nights customizing and customizing and drilling down into the system. Whew...its' like composing music. I get a big rush from creating this online universe of ours.

For many years, State of the Web was Happy Media's Internet News Outlet. We wrote some features on essential issues (ICANN and governance, various foibles and fiascos, Netsol, boom/bust, our own experiences, etc), aggregated some content, and put up some ads. Our News is now handled primarily through Daily Examiner, with a technology blog at Tech Toys.

What follows are some highlights of the analysis we published through State of the Web.

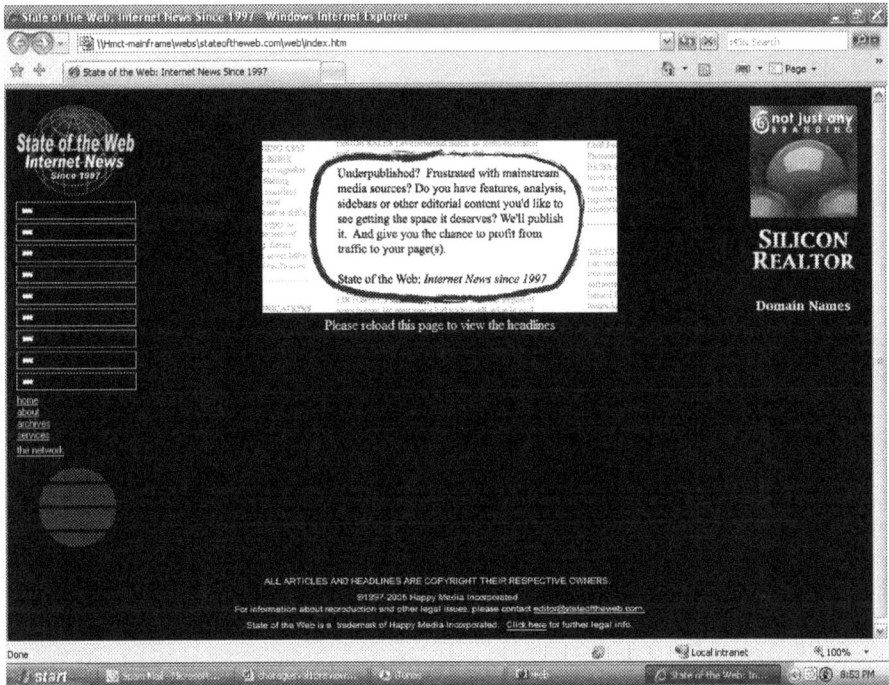

10/9/2006 11:26 PM

It's Back...

Just when we thought it was safe to have an intelligent discussion about Internet Business, the bright lights over at Google go all Old Media on us and buy the odious YouTube for 1.5 Billion.

My god. I thought that we, and the inexorable rush of time, had made it clear to everybody that some brand-of-the-minute that has a lot of eyeballs does not a business model make.

I'm not motivated by money. But there are some things that I would like that cost money. So I do hope that what we're doing...adhering to the principles of Resource Use Efficiency and Diversity of Sustainable Revenue Stream…eventually pays off. Harrumph.

It's just that, ultimately, we have a business model that works. We have a diversity of sustainable revenue streams, and we use our resources with unsurpassed efficiency. We just need to have more volume, whether it's traffic to our web sites, service clients, or property sales.

01.07.02 5 Predictions for 2002

1. More and more other companies will begin to talk about their "Network", although most will exist only in the mind of some Marketing geek.

2. At long last, the rest of the Internet industry will begin to recognize the difference between a company that's well-funded, and one that's well-run.

3. Advertisers will realize the limited value of those porn-inspired pop-up ads.

4. We will hear very little about new companies "destined to change the way we _____"

5. Two Words: More consolidation.

Stagnation, Outdated thinking, and Sheer Irresponsibility, Internet Style

07 July 2000

People like labels. Life's much easier if you can lump apples and oranges and kiwis in with all the other fruit. However, distinguishing what's under the labels often requires significantly more effort. Pretty much everyone has heard, in grade school science class, that a tomato, despite its presence in salads, is a fruit (because it has seeds). But does that make a cucumber a fruit too? What about a green pepper? With all this confusion in such a simple category like fruit, it is easy to sympathize with the members of the mainstream media who lately have been lumping all new media companies in with the currently out of favor "dot-coms."

However, we run a new media company, and I deeply resent the fact that conventional wisdom would have the temerity to lump my business in with what I've begun calling "Traditional Dot-Coms." The industry is so new, the technology and business ideas so cutting edge (or should be) that one might well wonder how we can add a "dot-com" to a term like "Traditional." Unfortunately, the moniker fits because many "dot-coms" have become just as formulaic in their approach to business in the New Economy, as the Old Economy behemoths they lambaste.

Here are some of the flaws inherent in companies that are representative of the "dot.com" bandwagon:

Fallacy #1: Promotional Strategy = Business Model

From <u>USA Today</u>

> *"Dropping the dot-com from our name will more accurately reflect our true business model of making every space an InfoSpace," CEO Naveen Jain says of the budding company in Bellevue, Wash.*

Every space an InfoSpace...hmm? And just how does trying to insinuate your company into every possible market constitute a "true business model?"

The name changes and the rebranding that happens so often amongst "traditional dot-com companies" have just about the same relationship to a "business model." Such strategies are not unique, nor do they aid in the development of really innovative methods of doing business; they are merely promotional strategies. For some unknown reason, the media often treat promotional strategies as business models, particularly when it comes to "dot-com" companies. One might wonder if this is just because the news media are too stupid to tell the difference, or if promotional strategies are all many companies really have to distinguish themselves.

For example, Happy Media's primary business model is to provide Corporate Quality B2B New Media services at below-market prices through a Network of sites and service companies, maintaining a healthy profit margin by the implementation of Maximum Resource Use efficiency, and the utilization of flexible, talented and affordable college-age labor.

This sort of business model is a far cry from many "dot-com" companies whose "business models" seem to include creating an unoriginal, single revenue-stream get-rich-quick idea for a website (as we've discussed in previous articles, a WEB SITE is not a web company), and then parleying that into millions of dollars worth of financing. Resources are then expended with gross irresponsibility on, amongst other things, extreme promotional schemes, designed to ingratiate these companies into the public consciousness, garner media attention, and propel the investment bloated start-ups to ill-fated IPO's like so many sinking ships. Unfortunately for many, the rats have gotten wise.

Fallacy #2:
Energy=Innovation;
"Experience"=New Economy Wisdom

From *LA Times*

> But in the current environment of skepticism and deeper scrutiny among the venture capital crowd, the bald and bespectacled Cross said he plans to use his experience to his advantage.
>
> The founder and chief executive of YourFreeStuff.com, an Internet portal to more than 700 offers of brand-name freebie merchandise on the Net, Cross was in Manhattan recently to tout the start-up to the financial and media worlds.
>
> It is difficult to imagine a less friendly environment for Internet-only start-ups, particularly for those whose primary business is, well, free stuff.

Since when can lack of revenue streams, a unique business model, or even a solid brand be made up for by "experience"? Today it seems that many innovative ideas are being crushed in a fury of Old Thinking. Responding to the "first to market" hysteria, the innovative is lost as those new ideas are plugged into outdated systems, wasting colossal amounts of money on things like Superbowl ads, rapid misdirected growth and bad promotional deals. Revenue streams, a strong brand, a viable business model, and a long-term strategy are swamped in the frenzy.

Fallacy #3: Money Grows on Trees

What the hell ever happened to the bottom line? To making sure that income doesn't exceed its expenditure? To good old-fashioned profits? What the hell ever happened to fiscal responsibility, keeping costs down, and resource use efficiency?

Once again, it's all been lost in a lot of Traditional Dot-Com hysteria. Fast money. Early retirement. Enormous wealth. And the great big fatted calf of all Traditional Dot-Coms, IPO. Maybe its time for companies to begin subscribing to a different philosophy, one of hard work, careful planning, maximization of resources and long-term business strategy development, over the long haul, with no hysteria.

??

Call us old-fashioned, but Happy Media has received only minimal financing, but the company is still paying the bills, and growing slowly but surely. Overhead is kept incredibly low through inexpensive labor and efficient use of limited resources. Happy Media may not blow up to become a multimedia supergiant with starry-eyed millionaire janitor/stockholders, but it won't wind up like the Titanic, either. Ten years from now, Happy Media will still be here.

Quick Reference:

Traditional Dot-Com Wisdom	Happy Media Wisdom
Must race to be first to market.	Spend the time to build a solid business model and develop strong customer relationships
Sell out to venture capitalists for funds to rent warehouse space, hire 200 employees, etc.	Provide quality service while building the company organically (slowly but steadily).
IPO or bust	Maintain profitability
Extreme expenditures now will be made up for by extreme profits later (or "I'll gladly pay you Tuesday for a hamburger today.")	Keeping overhead low and maintaining a steady but practical pace of growth will insure a strong company foundation on which to build

The Good Doctor is Bleeding My Economy Dry:

Resource Use-Efficiency in the 21st Century

27 June 2000

I remember C. Everett Koop's beard, from when I was a kid and he was the Surgeon General. If I'm not mistaken, it was on his watch that the government mandated warning labels on smokes. Fine work, General.

I've got a bit of a gripe, however, with how the man with the beard is spending his later years. You see, it's companies like the one that currently bears his name (DrKoop.com) that are spoiling the magical effect this fine new medium can have on our economy. It's not entirely fair to pick on the man, I know, because there are dozens, if not hundreds, of similar equity bandits operating equally, or even more leeching schemes. And his relationship with the "company" is really more of a licensing agreement than anything else. However, as one of the few fairly non-sinister public figures of the 80s, my warped sense of public service and community stewardship tells me that the man should look out for more than his own retired self.

Here's the skinny:

from Forbes

The fact that the health care information site had to issue a press release on Friday hailing a puny $1.5 million bridge loan from an unidentified merchant bank reeks of desperation.

and

The loan will keep Koop on its feet for only another month or so, according to Wit SoundView analyst Richard Lee. At the end of the first quarter, the site had about $8 million in cash, minus liabilities, and despite downsizing its spending $1.5 million to $2 million a month.

and

Dr.Koop.com may lack for content and visitors, but other company news that hasn't gotten any attention should help make the site an acquisition target anyway, according to Singer. That news is that the site's namesake, former U.S. Surgeon General Dr. C. Everett Koop, has agreed to continue lending his name and likeness to the site for seven more years. Since Koop owns an 8.3% stake in the company, this move to make the site more attractive to partners is clearly in his best fiscal interests.

The Koop brand, and the doctor's association with the site, are the only assets worth buying that DrKoop.com has left. "Without the aura of C. Everett, the site is worth nothing, so this commitment is mission critical for them to get a deal," says Singer. "This should allay the fears of any possible suitors [that Koop himself may abandon ship]."

Now maybe this makes my values old-fashioned, but I don't think it's right (although it's certainly natural) for even a marginally high-profile public servant, current or former, to deliberately sacrifice the overall health of the global economy for a quick buck.

Happy Media, the company that brings you State of the Web, currently spends approximately $12,500/month (when we have it). We're creating and incubating more than 150 web-based B2B and consumer services, vertical portals, and marketplaces. This Summer, we have a full-time staff of 8-10, with another 6-10 people working part-time, off-site, and in advisory roles.

Now, without question, our resource-use efficiency is by necessity. When my partner and I started this company in 1996, we had the shirts on our backs, and not much else. And while we've built The Network into something worth at least a few Hyundai's, we put every dime right back into the company. The end result? You guessed it...we've got a nice (cheap) office now, in the Thomas M. Quinn Memorial building, and a terrific, dedicated staff, about a dozen PCs, and not much else material to show for our efforts. Unless you count a few extra pounds, and a friendly new ulcer...

But we've been able to build the value of our company to 50 or 100 times what it was even one year ago. We've steadily added Intellectual Property, Web, Electronic and Physical resources to the point where we can outperform ANY SIMILAR operation in the vast majority of service areas, for a small fraction of the cost.

How does our organization maintain an extremely rapid rate of growth, with a non-existent budget? Not by marking up our prices, or robbing our customers of value in the services we provide, but by relying on Sweat Equity, motivating ourselves and our staff to perform at a higher level than any other enterprise would, and relying on a revolutionary Business Model.

Team Happy Media is anxiously awaiting the day when companies like ours, with Bottom Line Oriented Business Models, and a diverse network of Revenue Streams, will be receiving the bulk of VC and mainstream media attention. In terms of value to investor, client, corporate partner, and the economy as a whole, our way of doing business, in which resource use efficiency is placed above all else, brings considerably more to the table than some advertising-driven information space with a Celebrity Chairman of the Board.

Revenue Stream Diversity:
It's Not Just for Offline Anymore.

26 June 2000

All this talk of investors' "newfound skepticism" over various e-commerce sites' prospects for profitability is a real joke. Those of us not burdened by the weight of a "$240 million cash hoard" have been aware of the impending shakeout for quite some time.

Rather than dropping a few million on Superbowl ads, we've been spending the last 12 months expanding, diversifying, and streamlining our revenue streams. Companies like Happy Media have been anxiously awaiting the day when selling $1 bills for 96 cents, and trying to make up the difference with volume (see buy.com), or worse yet, spending $20,000,000/year to run a site with NO POTENTIAL REVENUE, other than advertising (see nearly every portal out there), will end. The process has already begun.

Proof that no company calling its employees "kosmonauts" will ever succeed in the US ...

> From Forbes:

> *The online delivery service, which specializes in one-hour delivery of products like soft drinks, burned through $26.3 million in 1999. To even approach the realm of profitability, Kozmo needs to dramatically increase its revenue--$3.5 million last year--by altering its business strategy.*

and

"The current business model, selling low-margin goods and delivering them for free, is not viable for the long term," says Rebecca Nidositko, senior analyst for online retail strategies at Yankee Group. "I don't think they have a model for profitability right now."

Sounds about right.

The simple fact of the matter is that a "web site", even one that sells a whole bunch of something, does not a "web company" make. Would it be considered wise to spend $20,000,000 to build and maintain a single brick-and-mortar pet store? Not likely. Yet somehow, in the band-wagon that was the late 90's, no less than a dozen companies did exactly that. I used to have a dog, and while at the time I decried the rising cost of pet food and other supplies, something tells me that it would take quite a few bags of IAMS and Eukanuba to pay just the rent, or just the executive salaries, of most of these irresponsible, 5th-to-market, VC bloated sinking ships.

The fantastic new medium, and the advancement in global commerce it has brought about, have not changed the basic fundamental principle of any business: Do not spend more than whatever products and services you offer can recoup in a reasonable period of time. While it's not crazy to spend a little over the top to gain initial market/mind share, or to promote a new venture, there simply isn't an adequate explanation for the fiscal irresponsibility still dominating this entire industry.

You make the call
(paraphrased from the Seattle Times)

*****.com had a little over $1 million in sales in 1999, but it lost $21.4 million. ****.com's Interim CEO declined to comment on the state of the company's financial health.*

*In January, it had about $9.6 million in cash, and **** chipped in $34.5 million in February to keep it afloat. With the employee count, now at about 180, and other development expenses rising, it had hoped to raise the needed capital in the stock market.*

Is this commercial juggernaut:

A) A tech company building the next generation web browser?
B) A B2B services company providing an integrated suite of small-business growth and management tools?
Or
C) "a Web hub for sites run by sports fans, publishers and merchants…?"

Alas, if you guessed "C," you get a gold star. One more time, for those of us who rode to school on the little bus: If you don't have any product or service to mark up above your costs, and the only thing you have to barter is advertising space…then the chances of your "company" being able to support any sort of 8-figure yearly overhead are extremely slim.

Client Life

We've mostly given up the client life. We have several dozen yearly subscription clients, mostly of the Internet Service (hosting, domain services, web mastering) variety. From the beginning of these ten years, our focus has been on more easily repeatable, if smaller, sources of revenue. Like this book, and our merchandise, and of course revenue from our low-operating-cost web sites.

It's a complicated issue, dealing with clients. As I made clear in the Introsurf, I am not a practical person. And while this most certainly translates into our providing superior value to each and every client, it also makes it rather more difficult to deal with clients that are, well, difficult.

We've provided Corporate, Creative, Internet, and Marketing Services to a very wide variety of clients. At this point, nothing ever really phases us, in terms of requests. And at the same time, it amazes us to see what sort of mess our fellow practitioners leave our new clients' web presence.

Here are short Case Studies of several of our favorite Clients. I think this group does a pretty good job of showcasing the wide range of people and organizations we work for (note: much of the text for this section comes directly from Client web sites):

ELISE MILLER

Elise's first novel, STAR CRAVING MAD, about a celeb-obsessed NYC private school teacher (Warner Books) is in stores now in the United States, Japan and Indonesia, and has been optioned for a movie by Lucky Crow Productions ("My Date With Drew"). Essays from her memoir, COCK-CRAZY! have been published on freshyarn.com, nerve.com, papotage.com and smallspriralnotebook.com. Her work has also appeared in The Sun Magazine. Elise has performed at Heeb Magazine's The Shmoth, and has read excerpts of her work in NYC and Brooklyn at Fez, Makor, HERE Arts Center, KGB, Boudoir Bar, Galapogos Arts Space and Halcyon.

Berklay Shipping

BERKLAY is a family-owned and operated, full service international freight forwarder, based at JFK AIRPORT (NY), with agencies worldwide. Established in 1965, by chairman

Bernard Klainberg, pioneer in air freight (formerly manager of Arista, ABC Freight, Panalpina (NY) 1953-1965).

- 3000 trade shows worldwide without loss or incident

- Over 1000 motorcycles and cars shipped since 1980

- Member, JFK Cargo Association (Includes US Customs, USDA, FAA, other government   agencies, airlines, forwarders, brokers and handling agents.)

- Located in the HEART of JFK AIRPORT, providing all import, export, domestic, warehousing, storage, packaging, containerization, and related services.

Scott Kreitzer

Hi Everybody! Welcome to my website, and thanks for visiting. In my travels, I get to do a variety of things. Sometimes it's a tenor sax solo on a jazz record...sometimes it's recording a vocal track that makes a lyric come alive. It's all very exciting work and I'm now glad to be able to share it with you. Any comments or questions would be most appreciated. Enjoy and come on in!

Since coming to New York from Miami in 1984, Scott has solidified himself, as being one of the top Saxophonists New York has to offer. Growing up in Florida gave Scott access to jazz legend Ira Sullivan, who quickly became Scott's mentor and employer as well. At 17, he toured with Ira's band around Southern Florida and performed regularly at the Café Exchange in Ft. Lauderdale. He then attended the University of Miami and finished his studies at William Paterson College in New Jersey. It was at William Paterson College that Scott began studying with Joe Lovano. He then went on to study with Bob Mintzer, only to be followed by a NEA grant to study with Eddie Daniels.

He is presently touring with the young sensation Peter Cincotti and only recently concluded the hit Broadway musical, Movin'Out. Scott is no stranger to the recording scene and has worked and produced for top bands and producers including the legendary Phil Ramone. Songwriting is a passion for Scott and in 1995 he had a #1 hit Single on Andy Snitzer's debut record and a top ten splash on the follow up record for Warner Brothers. After playing on six consecutive Spyro Gyra records, the groups leader sought out Scott's vocal songs for their 1995 release "Love and other Obsessions". ("Fine Time to Explain" and "Let's Say Goodbye")

Scott finds himself presently in Washington DC working on a new show soon to hit Broadway called "Hot Feet". Here we have the Music of Maurice White (Earth Wind and Fire) and the dance of Maurice Hines. This show may raise the bar yet even once again as Movin' Out moves over for a new funky urban treatment of "The Red Shoes". Stay tuned for future news posted here along with dates and links to help you see Scott up close or better yet maybe even on the big screen. By the way, yes that is Scott in Spiderman 2.

Kenneth J. Doka, Ph.D.

Dr. Kenneth J. Doka is a Professor of Gerontology at the Graduate School of The College of New Rochelle and Senior Consultant to the Hospice Foundation of America. A prolific author, Dr. Doka's books include *Pain Management at the End-of-Life: Bridging the Gap between Knowledge and Practice, Living with Grief: Ethical Dilemmas at the End of Life, Living with Grief: Alzheimer's Disease, Living with Grief: Coping with Public Tragedy; Men Don't Cry, Women Do: Transcending Gender Stereotypes of Grief; Living with Grief: Loss in Later Life, Disenfranchised Grief: Recognizing Hidden Sorrow: Living with Life Threatening Illness; Children Mourning, Mourning Children; Death and Spirituality; Living with Grief: After Sudden Loss; Living with Grief: When Illness is Prolonged; Living with Grief: Who We Are, How We Grieve; Living with Grief: At Work, School and Worship; Living with Grief: Children, Adolescents and Loss; Caregiving and Loss: Family Needs, Professional Responses; AIDS, Fear and Society; Aging and Developmental Disabilities; and Disenfranchised Grief: New Directions,*

Challenges, and Strategies for Practice. In addition to these books, he has published over 60 article and book chapters. Dr. Doka is editor of both *Omega* and *Journeys: A Newsletter for the Bereaved.*

Dr. Doka was elected President of the Association for Death Education and Counseling in 1993. In 1995, he was elected to the Board of Directors of the International Work Group on Dying, Death and Bereavement and served as chair from 1997-1999. The Association for Death Education and Counseling presented him with an Award for Outstanding Contributions in the Field of Death Education in 1998. In 2000 Scott and White presented him an award for Outstanding Contributions to Thanatology and Hospice. His *Alma Mater* Concordia College presented him with their first Distinguished Alumnus Award. In 2006, Dr. Doka was Grand-fathered in as a Mental Health Counselor under NY State's first licensure of counselors.

Dr. Doka has keynoted conferences throughout North America as well as Europe and Australia. He participates in the annual Hospice Foundation of America Teleconference, hosted by Cokie Roberts and has appeared on Nightline. In addition he has served as a consultant to medical, nursing, funeral service and hospice organizations as well as businesses and educational and social service agencies. Dr. Doka is an ordained Lutheran minister.

Lent Riker Smith Homestead

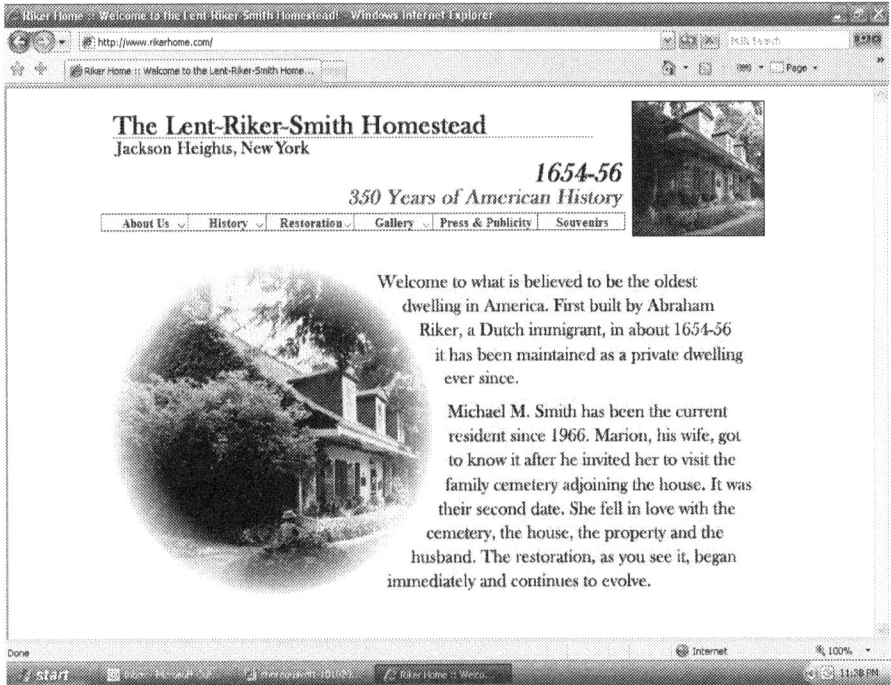

The Lent-Riker-Smith Homestead
Jackson Heights, New York

1654-56
350 Years of American History

About Us | History | Restoration | Gallery | Press & Publicity | Souvenirs

Welcome to what is believed to be the oldest dwelling in America. First built by Abraham Riker, a Dutch immigrant, in about 1654-56 it has been maintained as a private dwelling ever since.

Michael M. Smith has been the current resident since 1966. Marion, his wife, got to know it after he invited her to visit the family cemetery adjoining the house. It was their second date. She fell in love with the cemetery, the house, the property and the husband. The restoration, as you see it, began immediately and continues to evolve.

On August 9, 1654, Governor Peter Stuyvesant gave a patent certifying ownership of this land to Abraham Riker. The Lent-Riker-Smith Homestead was built in about 1656, according to the Historic American Buildings Survey. Major additions to the original Dutch farmhouse were made by Abraham Lent, a Riker descendant, about 1729. The house remained in possession of the Riker-Lent family until the 20th century, when it passed to William Gooth, who had been the personal secretary to the last Riker who owned the house. Gooth rented the house out to various tenants during the mid-

1900's, with the stipulation that nothing about the property could be changed.

Michael Smith has lived in the house since the 1960's. In 1975, he bought the property, the house and its contents from William Gooth. Beginning in 1980, he and his wife, Marion Duckworth Smith, began the present restoration.

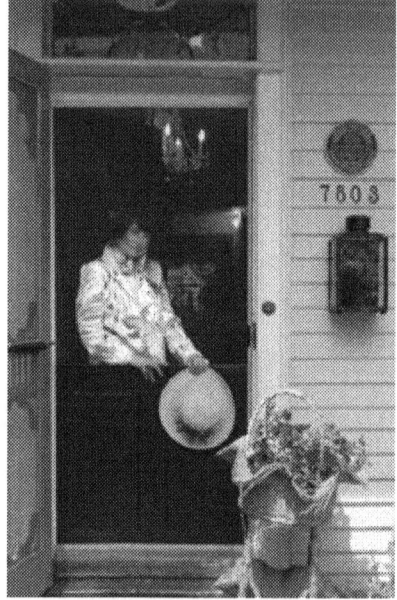

Mrs. Smith at the Front Door

The Riker Family graveyard in the rear contains 132 marked graves of the Rikers and the Lents. The exiled Irish Catholic patriot, Dr. William J. MacNeven, husband of Jane Riker, is buried here. Also buried here is Catherine Ann Tone, wife of Wolfe Tone, leader of the 1848 Irish revolt.

Ann Marie Ashton

Welcome!

Dutchess County is a great place to live. Centrally located between New York City and Albany; you'll appreciate many facets of our community: Employment Opportunities, Colleges,

Cultural Arts, Historic Sites, Recreation facilities and abundant natural beauty.

Credentials

Licensed Real Estate Broker

Certified New Home Specialist

Certified Relocation Specialist

Certified Mentor

Multi-Million Dollar Market & Sales Clubs

23 Years as a Realtor in Dutchess County

Affiliations

National Association of Realtors

Dutchess County Association of Realtors

Mid-Hudson Valley Multiple Listing Service

Next Market Strategies

Executive Bio: Mr. Bergman is a results-oriented sales and marketing executive with over 15 years of successful business development experience.

Involved in technology sales since 1989, when he started with DDC Publishing, he has consistently brought new products and services to market, led sales teams, opened up new distribution channels, sold to the Fortune 1000, built major client relationships, and boosted sales and profits for all the companies he has worked with.

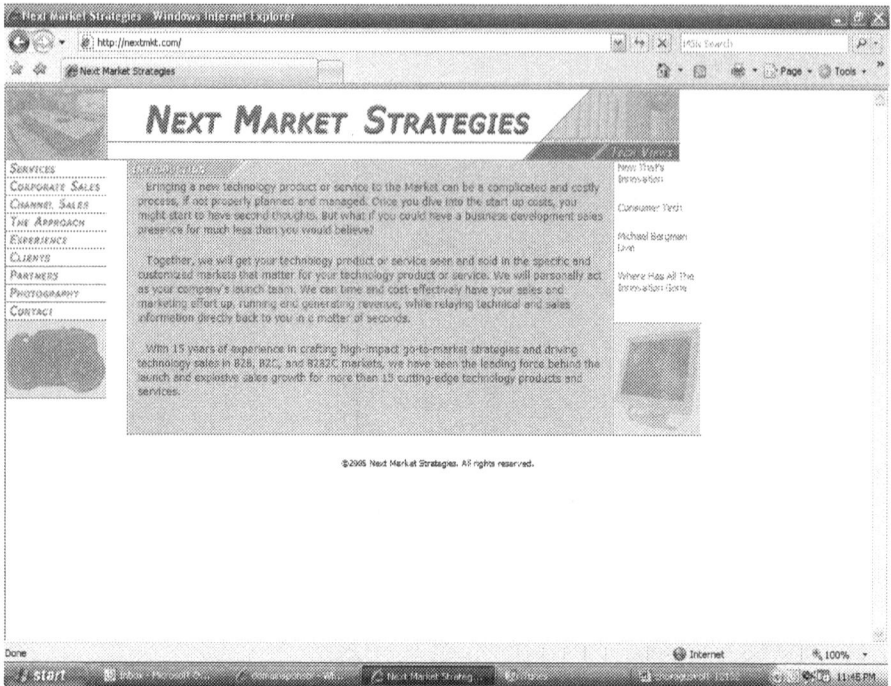

NEXT MARKET STRATEGIES

Mr. Bergman combines his innovative sales skills with a passion for results. He is a high-energy, focused executive, with a persuasive communication style.

He has led product development, marketing, sales, and implementation. He can successfully manage teams, as well as manage his own sales territory, redesigning processes, if needed, for greatest impact and results.

As a key contributor to his previous companies, Mr. Bergman has a proven record of launching technologies into new and untapped markets. A key sales researcher, he is able to uncover and correctly target potential prospect opportunities, either for direct sales or for sales through partnership channels.

He utilizes a unique grass-roots hunter approach to sales and marketing.

While with Channel Sources, Mr. Bergman created and orchestrated a master sales and marketing plan that outdistanced the competition and captured the #1 share in the voice recognition market for IBM Voice Systems. With New Generation Marketing, he delivered $23.2 million in aggregate new revenues to clients in a single year. Through his executive alliance-building skills, Mr. Bergman was able to forge strategic partnerships for Vendquest that resulted in the company's assets being favorably purchased by a major manufacturer.

In addition, Mr. Bergman is able to assist technology entrepreneurs and innovators in launching their new products into new markets. His approach has worked successfully by providing a framework to first find and define potential prospects, and then reach and persuade them in a cost-efficient and effective manner, keeping marketing costs low.

Literacy Event Productions

Literacy Event Productions organizes and promotes book sales for Libraries, Literacy Groups, Educational Groups and other charitable organizations.

Daily Examiner

Here are some highlights of our coverage of everything from the Toy Fair to the beginning of Ski Season. I started writing professionally when I was not yet a teenager. So by this time, more than 20 years later, I still enjoy turning a phrase, but lack the stamina to write at length. What I continue to do very well is edit, produce, massage, and punch up.

My family has been in the News business for a long time. My grandfather, Mark Sherwin, was the News Editor of the New York Post for many years. My father and other members of my family have written for the New York Daily News. I've written for the News, as well as The Berkshire Record, and an assortment of other publications.

That's why it's always gone without saying that any company of mine would have a News Outlet. When I was in the 4th grade, I started a newspaper for my class, the 210 News.

Daily Examiner provides original features, reviews, and commentary, as well as the latest headlines from more than 50 major online news outlets.   From Business News to Sports Scores to International Events and Politics, Daily Examiner has had the content you're looking for since 1998.

It's funny. We're developing so many properties, including web sites for more than 2 dozen non-profit and for-profit clients. In all of that, the fact that we own and operate our own online news source tends to get a little bit lost in the shuffle. It does not, however, diminish our pride in offering a fine mix of news sources for our audience, including headlines from more than 50 top online sources (CNN, NY Times, Reddit, to name a few).

What follows is a few highlights of our coverage in sports, technology and living. The first document that attests to the most fun the Daily Examiner team has ever had on an assignment. Early season skiing at Jiminy Peak in Massachusetts.

Early Season Delight: Jiminy Peak

12.01.2004 (Hancock, MA)

By Daily Examiner Staff

Our quest for an early start to our ski season in the east begins at Jiminy Peak in Hancock, MA. This North Western Massachusetts resort serves an average of 225,000 people a year, and is less than three hours from New York City and Boston, and just about an hour from Albany, NY, and Springfield, MA. This coming weekend (December 4 & 5) will be its fourth weekend of operation for the 2004/2005 Season.

The last leg of the drive was a very quick 45 minutes up from Great Barrington. After a quick stop for half of us at the rental shop, our snowboarders headed to the conveniently open novice hill, while the skiers took remarkable fast ride up the Berkshire Express, a High Speed Detachable "Sixpack". Later in the year Jiminy will unveil its new for 2005 terrain park and halfpipe, as well as 4 new trails, 2 improved trails, and the Maloney Ski Patrol Building.

"This early in the season," says Sally Johnstone, Head of Marketing, in characteristic straightforwardness, "it's not perfect." Hey, to be honest, it's too cold to play golf, so skiing in

Southern New England is a perfect idea. On the drive from New York this Thanksgiving, you wouldn't have seen a single snowflake on the ground or in the air. But here on Saturday at Jiminy the six of us (4 on skis/2 on snowboards) found plenty enough snow to enjoy a full day of skiing, early season physical conditioning permitting. Several of us have not been up on the mountain much in the past few years, but all of us have enjoyed skiing for many years at varying skill levels.

Jiminy accurately bills itself the largest Winter Sports Center in Southern New England. It boasts 43 trails covering 170 acres, with plenty of variety and volume for any skill level. The mountain has been open for business since 1948, the last 35 years under the careful attention of owner Brian Fairbank. Katie Tworek, Special Events Coordinator, summed it up thusly:

"This is his passion. It's so good to have someone who's here every day, and who really cares about it."

93% of the mountain is covered by an impressive snowmaking system. On Jiminy Peak's Opening Day November 13th, it had 9 trails open from the top. And it was clear to all of us that this was not the snowmaking of our youth. Less than 48 hours after a positively balmy Thanksgiving Day, the trails that were open were very well covered throughout the day (other than a few unavoidable grass/slush areas).

A warm Happy Media welcome to the newest member of the Jiminy family - Dalton Guy, weighing in at 9 lbs 13 ozs and 22 inches long! We wish Dalton, Sally, and the rest of the Jiminy Team a Happy and Healthy Holiday Season!

* * *

American International Toy Fair
By Greg Anastos
Daily Examiner July 2003

What is the American International Toy Fair? Do they have fair toys? What are un-fair toys? I will answer the last question first. Those are the toys you can't afford. Now, there is no such thing as a fair toy because we can all cheat. As for what is the American International Toy Fair, that is what this report is all about.

The Javits Center is a beautiful place. I've never been to it before, so I was excited when the opportunity came up for me to attend. It was a bit of a trek to get there since I live in Astoria but one trip with the N-train and a bit of walking and bam! There I was.

I wondered around a bit, trying to get my footing, and more importantly, my press pass or they wouldn't let me in to the fair. After I got my credentials, it was off to adventure.

My eyes gazed around looking at all the colorful banners and displays. I thought that if any colorblind people are here, they must have been having a hard time. Anyway, I began walking around and looking at the booths and studying their wares. You'd be amazed at how serious these people are. It's an interesting contrast to see all these fun and colorful toys and standing next to them are so many people in 3-piece suits looking very serious. I guess toys are fun to buy and play but not always fun to play and market. My criteria for judging the toys was simple:

Quality: Is it made well? Are the materials long lasting and eye catching?

Interesting: Would I like to play with them or start a collection? Would other people my age and gender or the opposite or younger or older people like these things as well? I had to use my imagination a lot on that one.

And more importantly, are they easy to use and easy to learn? Nothing is more frustrating than a toy or a game that takes an I.Q. of 200 or more to understand. Luckily for me and other fellow press people and buyers, press kits provided by the exhibitors made life for everyone easier. These are my top ten (ams note…we've printed the top 5 here) favorites. Here we go:

5. Pyramat300 (www.pyramat.com) Now I'm down to the top five and the Pyramat300 deserves to be in the top five. It's a full body mat that you can lie down on and it has a headrest with built-in 2 25-watt speakers and a 4-inch woofer. You can connect up to 8 of them and everyone feels the full impact of the games they are playing at the same time. On the back of the headrest, there are 2 RCA female-to-female adapters built in, and a 9-pin detachable hard remote so you have total control and not have to get up. The best for the hard core gamer.

4. Playmobil (www.playmobil.com) Who can resist Playmobil. It was RPG and the Sims before RPG and the Sims. You can create whole communities and even a society with it. Pirates, Knights, Vikings, etc. Or even regular modern communities with homes and police, fire departments, construction, etc. Playmobil 2004 has all this and now more. New features, like RC, where your trains and cars can now be controlled with a remote control. It's the ever-growing Playmbil universe. For toddlers and up to young children.

3. Flashback (www.flashbackgames.com) Yet another board game but cooler. It's nostalgia time and this game has it in spades. There are two different editions, movie and sitcom. The home version's have 800 playing cards in 2 decks (3,200) a game board and 4 playing pieces. Travel editions include 400 playing cards in 1 card deck (1,600 questions) a scoring pad and pencil. You move across the board without a die or a variation of it. It's the difficulty of the question that dictates how far ahead you get. The harder the question, the more spaces you can move. The easier the question, the lesser spaces you can move. Lot's of fun.

2. Scalextric (www.scalextric-usa.com) Racing is universal among guys. The challenge, speed, sense of danger, and of course, having a cool, fast car! Scalextric takes it to a whole other level. I had a racing set when I was a kid. I just had to connect the track, plug it in and the cars would go round and round. The cars had some stickers on them and you were happy that the toy makers put some detail on them. But Scalextric is different. Full working headlights and rear lights, the cars are built to 1:18 scale and a metallic paint finish. You can race with them or collect them. The limited edition versions of the cars come with a photo-etched plaque on the underpan and come in a presentation case with an individually number certificate of authenticity. A variety of tracks keep the race varied with jump options, criss-cross over each other racing, sharp curves and more. Go to the website and see for yourself. Too many options to fit here.

1. Sideshow Collectibles (www.sideshowcolectibles.com) Now we come to the end of our journey. Where this intrepid reporter chooses his #1 favorite at the Toy Fair. Sideshow Collectibles makes the best movie/T.V. tie-in figures I have ever seen. The detail and lifelike look of the figures is impressive. This year they had plenty of recent movie and T.V. characters and even classic ones as well. The horror characters collection first grabbed my eyes. Freddy Krueger, Michael Meyers, Jason Vorhees and Leatherface have been re-created as 12" figures. They have real fabric clothing and the life-like detail were preserved. Like some mad wizard put a spell on them and shrunk them down to 1' high. At night, I'd keep them locked in a case if I was you. Other recent editions include T.V.'s Buffy, the Vampire Slayer, Angel, X-Files, R. Lee. Ermey (from the movie Full Metal Jacket) but not as the film character. Here he is as himself from his hit show "Mail Call" on The History Channel. It comes as a talking figure with R-Rated and Xtra-Salty language. YES! No P.C. crap here. Just pure military honesty. Other re-creations include Civil War historical figures, WWI, WWII, Western, and more. Now to my truly favorite ones. Vintage movie and T.V. characters! First the movies. From Universal Studios Classic monster movie days they have re-created Count Dracula, The Wolfman, and Frankenstein's Monster. Once again, all 12" high with real fabric clothing and great detail. Other characters included are The Phantom of the Opera, Mr. Hyde, Nosferatu the Vampyre and the great silent but lost film, "London after Midnight", Lon Chaney's "Vampire". From classic T.V. you have some of the famous aliens from "The Outer Limits" like Ebonite guard, Ikar and Ikar's soldier and the super-evolved human, Gyllan. Great stuff. From "The Twilight Zone" you have the Gremlin from the episode, "Nightmare at 20,000 feet" with William Shatner, deformed doctors from "Eye of the Beholder", The Invader from the episode, "The Invaders" and Kanamit (14" tall) from the episode, "To Serve Man". I want to get them all! Go to their site and see even more that I can't cram into this article. All great stuff!

So that's it toy fans. The top ten of the fair. I believe I've chosen some of the best of the best. So farewell for now, and remember, "Play Nice".

If Only Computers Were Only Like TVs

by Richard Sherwin

Daily Examiner Aug 2003

My old boss was a veteran of the consumer electronics industry. He was a journalist/early tech adopter who, literally, brought back the first tiny transistor radios from Japan. Right before he retired, he made some startling comments for a guy who quite literally had a part in starting the CE industry.

About 20years ago, he was told by our younger editorial staff that the computer industry was starting to add TV/movie like video and higher quality audio to the computer screen, along with animation and pictures. This content would be on new compact disks or could be transferred to your home PC in several ways. Dubbed "multimedia", it would be played back on your laptop or home computer screen which was, at that time, smaller than today's standards screens.

The venerable editor in chief said, "Wow! What are those great Silicon Valley engineers going to think of next? Pretty soon, they'll discover television and radio... And when they do, are the engineers going to be as irresponsible as they are now with software programs that won't work, totally unreliable hardware and customer support almost non existent?

"And, more importantly, are these things going work when your really need them? Will they be so easy to operated, that the entire family – including grandma – will be able to watch/do want they want, changing channels or content when they want? Like TV?"

"If they (the PC guys) do as bad a job with the reliability and ease of use, that they've shown to date, then there's nothing they can discover or invent that will impress me."

My old boss was right. Hardly any of these devices is as reliable or as easy to use as your TV or radio.

When my boss also learned a few years later that some PC companies (software and hardware) were not including printed directions with their $40 - $4,000 devices, and that many consumer electronics companies were telling their customers that Customer Service and instructions were now mainly available on the Internet with very little telephone support, well he just walked away…and retired.

He would be even more disturbed to learn that today some of the best innovations in software and hardware come not from the big manufacturers themselves but from "shareware or freeware" created by frustrated customers to make their devices work better.

But my old boss' biggest fear is coming to fruition, too. Now it's not just computers. TV and radio manufacturers, cable TV companies and broadcasters are forced (either by Microsoft or the ubiquities of home computers) to make their devices and reliant on computer technology.

He used to mutter, "Can you ever think that people will have to wait for their TVs or radios to boot up? Could you ever think we would have to "reset" our TV and radios…?

The moral of this story is that the other day, he called me to complain that his cable company added a new set-top box to his system and he (after urging from his family) purchased a TIVO personal video recorder.

"I couldn't start watching TV until the cable box went through computer like boot-up gyrations. When that was finished, I plugged in the so called second generation TIVO and that, too had to boot-up.

"You know that old saying, KISS (which means Keep It Simple Stupid)? I guess nobody believes that anymore."

*　　*　　*

Good Homes

I've been, at long last, after 10 years in New York, finally been put out to pasture. My wife and I have moved to CT and I've set up Happy Media's first outpost in that state. As part of that move, Happy Media has launched V1 of LitchfieldCT.org, wherein I'm hoping to duplicate the Community Stewardship efforts that have so marked our continuing presence in Astoria, NY.

You may find that a few of your favorite Happy Media properties are pointed to more generic content than usual. We apologize for any inconvenience. These Paid Parking Programs are the most efficient way to generate at least some revenue from every single property. Drop us a line anytime to discuss what properties you'd most like to see switched back towards Original Content.

Good Homes® is one such web site. When active, it's a Real Estate Directory, one of our most popular sites. We provide categorized real-estate listings for all 50 states and much of the rest of the world, as well as links to financing, home building, and other resources. Here are some highlights of our listing over the years:

Brick Split Foyer (8 yrs. old)
Clinton, MD 20735
Listing Price: $225,000
This exceptional brick split foyer is located on a great lot just across the street from scenic Cosca Park in Clinton in the Boniwood Neighborhood. This neighborhood is conveniently located near AAFB, Metrorail, Metrobus, the Capital Beltway and is only a short commute to DC.

Prime Park-like Location
Rye, NY 10580
Listing Price: $365,000
Spacious, sunny & quiet 1,100sf 2BR, 1BA coop in beau tudor bldg. LR w/FP, DR, EIK w/granite countertop, hdwd flrs, WR/DR in unit, beach rights, 38 mins Xpress to NYC, easy walk to town, train, beach/parks, golf, & schools. Pets OK.

Great Starter Home

Worth, IL 60482

Listing Price: $159.000

Bedrooms have combined walk-thru closet, 10x10 back porch, privacy fenced large backyard, garage is heated w/320 elec line

Ext: vinyl sided w/crawl space & large attic

Appliances: gas stove, refrig and washer/dryer

Great starter home, near schools and public transportation

Open House 3/21 11-4

Van Nuys West, CA 91406

Listing Price: $435000

Charming remodeled light and bright California traditional w/ large pool sized backyard on quiet pride of ownership street. New paint in/out, updated kitchen and bath, new central A/C & Heat, beautiful refinished hardwood floors, Living Room with fireplace. new light fixtures throughout, lots of storage and closets, crown molding, beautifully landscaped, large covered patio. Vacant.

Well Kept

Susanville, CA

Listing Price: $194500.

Well kept and clean home on private corner lot in the pine trees. Beautiful redwood deck, great for relaxing or entertaining. Separate laundry room off kitchen with large pantry. Open floor plan oversized 2 car garage with work bench.landscaped front and back.

4BR/ 2.5BA in Quiet South Natomas Cul-de-sac

Sacramento, CA 95833

Listing Price: $288900

With Master Retreat & 2 car garage. Close to schools, shopping, and downtown. 2-story, CH/A, fireplace, whole house fan, hot tub/jacuzzi and security system. Attractive landscaping includes 28 dwarf fruit trees, blueberries, strawberries, grapes, redwood deck w/ gazebo, vegetable garden area, herb garden w/ fountain, and 17-foot indoor fishtail palm tree included!

FSBO: *Beach Luxury in Single Family Home.*

Boca Raton, FL

Listing at $579,000

4 Bedroom, two bath with Master suite. Luxury Master bath. All rooms open to lovely pool area. Stone tile throughout. Neutral and peaceful! One block to sunny Boca Raton Beach! Close to historic Downtown Boca! Perfect for professionals, family or retired couple!

FSBO: Lakeshore and 2 Cabins on Cedar Lake

Near Ely, Minn.

Listing Price: Make an Offer

Beautiful 1.5 Acre Point including Cabin and smaller Log Cabin right next to the lake. Fantastic Fishing Lake! Gorgeous Point! HURRY.... this listing won't last long!!

Fairmount Neighborhood 40s Classic

Eugene, OR

Listing Price: $369000

4 Bedrooms (or use very large downstairs bedroom as a family room) 2 baths. Downstairs bath has large, tiled, walk-in shower Beautiful mahogany central wall and new, quarter-sawn, red oak floors Architect-designed third bedroom and deck Professionally installed native plant garden (now about two years old) Established landscaping, built-in irrigation system 2 Fireplaces

4 Bed/2 Bath

Silver City, NM 88061

Listing Price: $119,900

Walking distance to downtown and WNMU. A stone's throw from Jose' Barrios and the Virginia St. Park. Corner lot on quiet street with homeowner neighbors. At 2400 sq. feet., this versatile space with new updates can serve as a single or dual family residence. The original house is a three bedroom, one bath with a living/dining area and extra large family room which opens onto a patio. This part of the house is connected to a beautiful five-year-old apartment with a private entrance and courtyard.

WELL CARED-FOR HOME
South Williamsport, PA 17702
Listing Price: $135,900
FEATURING Modern updated kitchen and baths with, new appliances, Cherry kitchen cabinets, hardwood floors, Elegant fire place in living room with gas insert, First Floor laundry with new stackable washer and dryer, Formal dinning room, Four bedrooms, Huge attic, Divided basement with workout area, Paved drive and parking area, Double glazed vinyl replacement windows, Front porch overlooking view of river, Rear Patio

On 120 acres
Tomah, WI 54660
Listing price: 495,000
Relax in the country on 120 acres with a very scenic view. Also includes a farm house, barn, pole sheds, silo, granary, and several other storage buildings in good condition.

FSBO: HUGE COLONIAL
Teaneck, NJ 07666
Listing Price: $349900

HUGE COLONIAL House on a desirable street, close to shopping schools, movies and houses of worship...it's a great neighborhood. Patio, above ground pool (can be removed), fenced yard professionally landscaped, hard wood floors (all natural chestnut woodwork), 2 matching stained glass windows, and more.

FSBO: 93.5 Acres with two homes.
San Augustine, TX
Listing Price: Unknown

Large covered back porch overlooking pasture, woods, pond. Pole barn and tractor shed. Bordered by two creeks. Second home is 1996 3/2 doublewide - for guests, mother-in-law, or rental. Could be sold to off-set price. Near Sam Rayburn and Toledo Bend reservoirs in the Deep East Texas Piney Woods. Plenty of privacy, but only about three miles from town.

Former Model Home
Las Vegas, NV
Listing Price: $245,000

Former new model listed by motivated seller. High energy star home ready for immediate move-in. Open floor plan. Kitchen with nook and island, granite countertops, hickory wood cabinets with pull-outs and pantry. Large master bedroom with fireplace, large walk-in closet, sitting room with shelves, private bath and door to patio. Two additional large bedrooms, one with built-in cabinets and shelves and large walk-in closet. Separate formal dining area and living room. Vaulted ceilings with fans. Intercom system and alarm system complete. Professionally landscaped in front and back on automatic watering system. Close to shopping and schools.

Electronic Real Estate

I'll be honest with you. If we can get some more action on these properties, get this machine generating 10-20k/month from traffic and links alone…you'll never hear from me again. No more Weekly Update, no more Choragus, no more Adam's Notes…well, maybe I'd still write my notes. And of course I'd still publish Daily Examiner, and do all of our Community Stewardship work. Just no more typing.

I honestly believe that our properties are valuable and viable enough to eventually make us that sort of dough. And while I do enjoy having written…the sitting here and grinding out paragraphs is just deadly. Here I am, maybe a month after writing the rest of this paragraph, just now getting to the editing and cleaning portion of our program. And again, now, a week or so later, as I return to this very same section.

Anyway, as I've mentioned, **Happy Media**® owns a large portfolio of corporate-quality domain names, business identities, web sites, and operational businesses. We have developed what we feel is some of the very best electronic real estate on the Internet. We have been involved in the divestiture of:

Gofish.com, Dogood.org, PitchIt.com, FOOP.com, JustPeople.com, iSherpa.com, Justpeople.com, Vixo.com, Elbrujo.com, Bastante.com, muyrico.com, Digitalarmada.com, Domainshark.com, Thebigdeal.com, Carboncycle.com, Swingcam.com, Newtomorrow.com, Fastbucks.com, Cyberswing.com, factbase.com, goodvibe.com, strongfuture.com, Getcurrent.com, Discfactory.com

Most recently, just as I'm finishing up this manuscript (11/06...now 12/12), we've sold fastclips.com and luxurysuite.com, helping us to get all of our ducks in a row for the quickly approaching new year. And allowing me, at last, a bit of peace in which to work on these pages for you folks.

Click here
To schedule your
free consultation

We have more than 250 individual internet properties available for our continued development, and that of our clients. We've provided superior service to more than three dozen clients from all over the world. Our Electronic Real Estate is of the highest quality, and ready for development. Prices range from $1999 to $100,000. Businesses in need of a Superior Quality Corporate Identity, Trademark, Domain Name, Business Plan or other

Intellectual Property, need look no further.

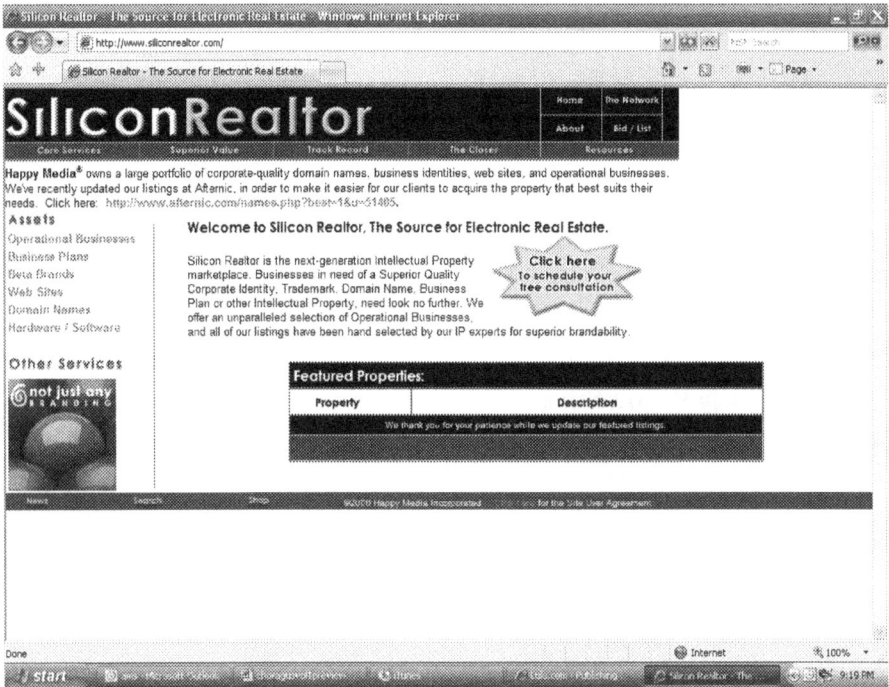

So if you're looking to break into a new industry, take over and manage an existing business, or if you just need to get your hands on a prime piece of Electronic Real Estate, Happy Media should be your primary source for the Electronic Real Estate necessary to begin building a modern business.

Some Highlights of our Holdings

360nyc Live Music Blog	www.360nyc.com
Archivore Backup Solutions	www.archivore.com
Access Road Internet Services	www.accessroad.com
Accubill Accounting	www.accubill.com
Amplitone Records	www.amplitone.com
beautiful world creations	www.beautifulworld.com
Betabrand Corporate Identity Services	www.betabrand.com
Brand Shield IP Protection	www.brandshield.com
Bursar.com Education Funding	www.bursar.com
Crosskick Soccer	www.crosskick.com
Creepy Crawly Halloween Superstore	www.creepycrawly.com
Careguard Safe Search	www.careguard.com
Cash Flash Financial Services	www.cashflash.com
cryptomagic security	www.cryptomagic.com
Cyberhug Online Greetings	www.cyberhug.com
Daily Examiner News Center	www.dailyexaminer.com
Debitron Electronic Wallet	www.debitron.com
documo desktop publishing	www.documo.com
Domainsmith ®	www.domainsmith.com
Educafe Learning Center	www.educafe.com
Ego Boost - Feel better about yourself.	www.egoboost.com
Fact Bank Data Center	www.factbank.com
Filmville Productions	www.filmville.com
Good Homes® Real Estate	www.goodhomes.com
Globego Travel Center	www.globego.com
Great Servers High-End Hosting	www.greatservers.com
Gymbest Exercise Equipment	www.gymbest.com
Honey Oats...mmmmm.	www.honeyoats.com
Hitcraft Traffic Acceleration	www.hitcraft.com
hypnologic guerilla marketing	www.hypnologic.com
Intranova Business Architecture	www.intranova.com
ideaNIC DNS Services	www.ideanic.com
icantina Web Cafe	www.icantina.com
The Libertarium	www.libertarium.com
Local Bonus	www.localbonus.com

Lucky Shot Human-Edited Web Directory	www.luckyshot.com
Main Concourse Online Mall	www.mainconcourse.com
mxur dj	www.mxur.com
Media Mile Entertainment Store	www.mediamile.com
Metrique	www.metrique.com
Monetary Standard	www.monetarystandard.com
MindCAM Presentations	www.mindcam.com
not just any Branding	www.notjustany.com
NETUNITE Community	www.netunite.com
neoluna creations for women	www.neoluna.com
Let's go Out to Dinner	www.outtodinner.com
Omnidef Records	www.omnidef.com
Pharmagia Online Health Center	www.pharmagia.com
Profitron Affiliate Marketing	www.profitron.com
Power Brunch Business Networking	www.powerbrunch.com
Portable Worker	www.portableworker.com
Promodome Promotional Products	www.promodome.com
Priceflex Marketplace	www.priceflex.com
Que Suerte - What Luck!	www.quesuerte.com
Quora Market Research	www.quora.com
Real Estate New York City	www.renyc.com
Rushjob Business Services	www.rushjob.com
Skillmax® Testing Services	www.skillmax.com
Silicon Realtor IP Marketplace	www.siliconrealtor.com
Superbody Fitness	www.superbody.com
Staffwire Human Resources	www.staffwire.com
The Big Check	www.thebigcheck.com
Trustwell Insurance	www.trustwell.com
Topsy Turvy Toys and Things	www.topsyturvy.com
Tech Toys Electronics	www.techtoys.com
Unigent Turn Key Solutions	www.unigent.com
Warelock Security	www.warelock.com
Whomp Sports	www.whomp.com
whyMEDIA Designs	www.whymedia.com
Wonderbot	www.wonderbot.com
Wrenchy	www.wrenchy.com
ZwaP gAMING	www.zwap.com

Weekly
Update

Weekly Update comes out…well, 20 or 30 times a year. In fact, as we speak I'm looking at a 30 Day Monthly Planner that shows just one WU sent out this month thus far, and 2 more boldly scheduled for the last two Mondays of the month.

And now, as I'm revising and editing this section (about 3 weeks later), it's late December and we've sent out a single newsletter this month. Yesterday we featured a striking, just received new email (which I think we helped create) from ASAP, a human rights organization with whom we work.

Since 1999, this newsletter has been providing its subscribers with the latest developments in the always rapidly

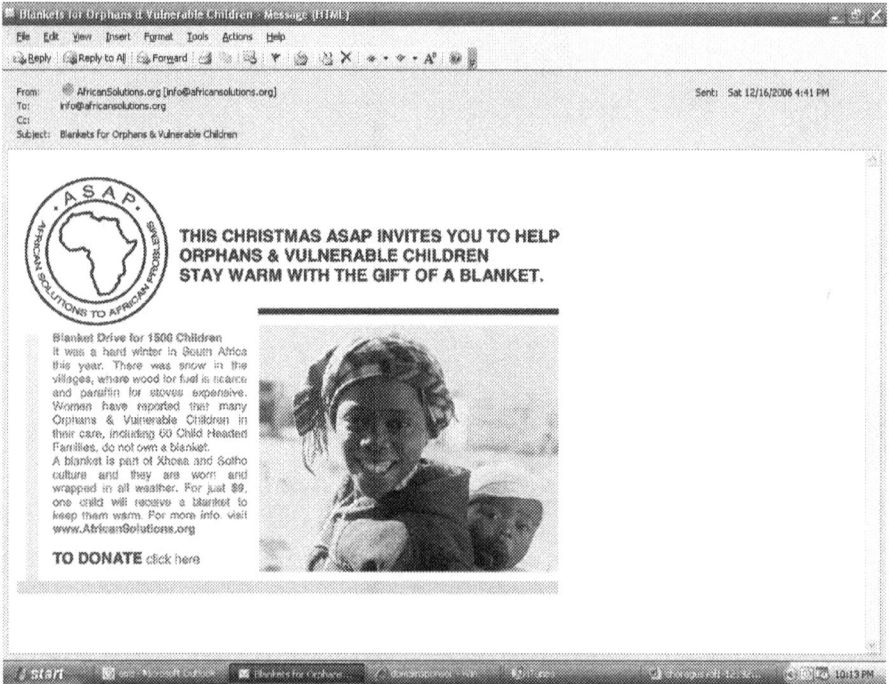

expanding Happy Media universe, as well as the Internet, New Media, and Business communities at large.

Each Edition is different, but you'll see a lot of features about our various Non-Profit and Community Partners, as well as quick looks at many of our more interesting clients, and Happy Media owned properties. This can mean anything from plays and musicals and literature, to sporting events and musical releases, as well as a truly vast assortment of business-to-business services.

By which we mean domain registration, web hosting, web mastering, graphic design, promotional materials, market research, corporate naming and branding, and general business and Non-Profit consulting.

Within what I do, there's a lot of creating while creating. For example, in the process of creating the newsletter, I frequently have to write some short rifs of punchy copy about our various web sites, projects, partners, and so on. In doing so, I very often write stuff that is better than what's already on the materials for the web site or project to which I've referred. This copy gets put on the web site or other materials, which reminds me vividly how this whole thing works. Which suggests to me that I sit down, and write this out for you good folks. See?

Wow…this first one is an old one. From the days just after we moved into our suite of office in the Thomas M. Quinn Memorial Building. It still amazes me that we were able to get that space in the first place, and do as much as we did with it. For the most part, we were too busy building the bedrock core properties of our Network to do much promotion at that point. Oh, and hacky sack.

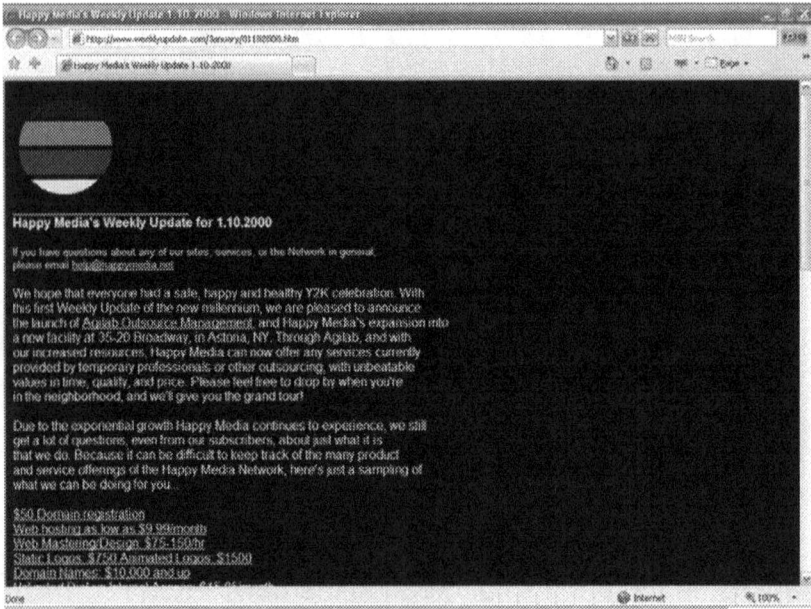

Happy Media's Weekly Update for 10.11.1999

A brief note about the current status of the network, as well as our plans for the future:

Since its incorporation in April of 1997, Happy Media has generated 28% profit on expenditures that would likely fall short of the office-supply budget of any other small company. No salaries have been paid, and all monies have been re-invested in the company. To this date, Happy Media Incorporated has received zero seed money, venture capital, loans, or other financing.

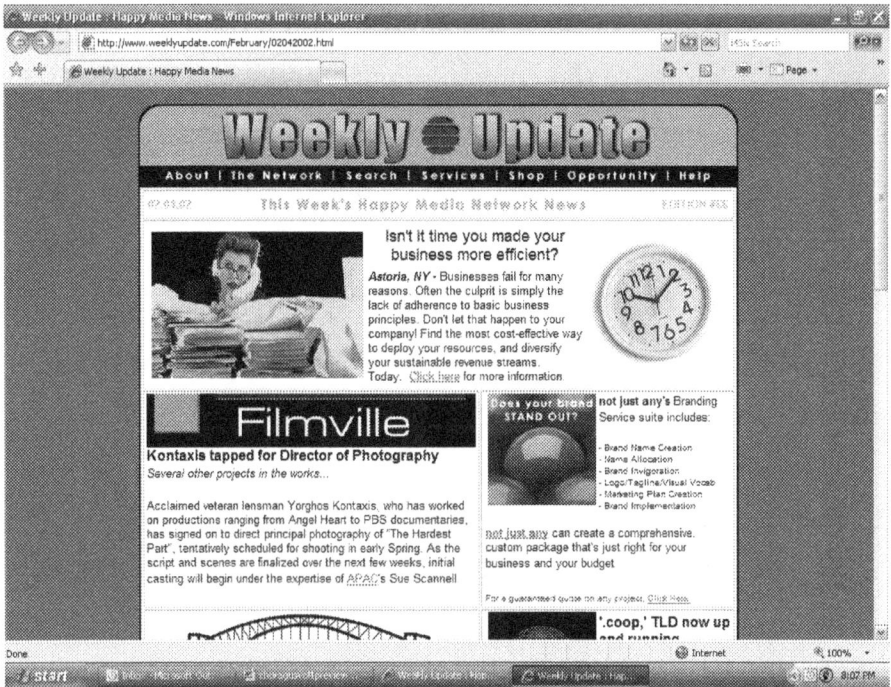

As such, the sites and related services that will make up the Network are being built piece by piece. Most of the live sites are at about 15-30% of full operation, and while a few are at 30-50% of their planned state, the majority of our eventual sites exist only on our local intranet, as we build them for your future use. Each member of working in excess of 100 hours a week as we attempt to address this matter, and in the next weeks and months you will continue to see a remarkable rate of growth in the quality and quantity of both the sites themselves, and our preparedness to provide the related services.

Our staff has tremendous faith in the business model Happy Media is executing (mostly due to the response we receive from the public and our members), and that an investment in any of Happy Media's brand(s) is sure to generate substantial returns in the coming months and years. As such, we welcome inquiries, suggestions, and referrals from any interested potential partners, both corporate . Similarly, we are looking for contract employees from both the virtual village, and the NYC area. Obviously, all proposals will be evaluated on a case-by-case basis...but we look forward to working with many of you in the future.

Thanks again for all your support!

Team Happy Media

Happy Media's Weekly Update for 4.11.2000

If you have questions about any of our sites, services, or the Network in general, please email help@happymedia.net.

Team Happy Media was able to celebrate our third anniversary with a smile yesterday, as NotJustAny Corporate Identity Services http://www.notjustany.com successfully provided yet another superior brand to another satisfied client. The celebration allowed our staff the opportunity to reflect on the amazing growth of the company and to focus on the future, as we continue moving full speed ahead in developing our ever-burgeoning stable of businesses.

The continued growth of Happy Media's staff and resources has allowed the executive staff some time to plan ahead for the company's upcoming expansion. As our brands organically develop, and our staff size follows suit, the company will be in need of a great deal more space in six months to a year. Currently, we are in the process of pricing a number of production facilities ranging from 12,000 to 40,000 square feet, all within the Astoria/Long Island City borders.

For this week, our concentration returns to building up and polishing the core brands. Check out Why?MEDIA Designs http://www.whymedia.com, as our Graphic Design shop will be going through a complete make-over this week due to the overwhelming success of last week's Banner and Logo campaign. Minor positive changes are also in the works at http://www.elbrujo.com, our alternative medicine and health site, and http://www.stateoftheweb.com, which now has an archive of our features, in addition to bringing you the latest web news.

In addition, Happy Media's corporate site http://www.happymedia.com, will be transforming for the second time in as many weeks. Now that we have a good deal more of our brands on display, we will follow with an appropriate portal site that is both informative, and user-friendly. Look for it by Friday. Lastly, due to NotJustAny's growing list of clientele, we feel the site deserves a revamp. A brand new logo, combined with updated content and a more stylistic format, will further NotJustAny's reputation as a serious competitor in the Corporate Identity marketplace. Stay tuned for this and many other cosmetic improvements.

Network Status Update

Banner and Logo week, which culminated on Saturday, turned out to be even more successful than we had ever imagined. We now have graphically superior logos for nearly all of our core brands, and a wide range of banners to guide viewers between our numerous sites. Surf the Happy Media Network for a glimpse of the results!

And, our diligent search engine submission is beginning to pay off. With NotJustAny leading the way, Happy Media's brands are beginning to pop up on the majority of the thirty most popular search engines. AltaVista has been especially prompt in their work, and many of Happy Media's brands are coming up in the top three for certain keyword searches on their site.

Until next week, Be well.
Team Happy Media

P.S. Happy Media is currently building its summer internship program. If you know of anyone who is interested in learning the ins and outs of business in the new economy, have them e-mail interns@happymedia.com or call us at 718.726.3901, and ask for Nico.

Power Brunch

We've had three Power Brunches. The first, in 2001 was attended by 11 people, including 2 Happy Media people and 1 person who came to the event by accident. The second, in 2002, featured better food, 2 Speaking Authors, a Photographic Art Exhibit, and was attended by about 35 people. The third, in 2003, had readings by Ned Vizzini and Elise Miller, Original Artwork by Nicole Mazur and Nick Friedman, free Happy Media Gear, the Best Bagels in Queens, and was attended by about 50 people.

Here's a short, funny story about the hubris of youth, especially Happy Media youth:

I was in "The Big Space", moving some furniture. It was cold, and since "The Big Space" wasn't actually under our lease, and thus had no heat. I was cycling some of our desk/tables from the mostly unused "Big Space" to our Office Suite proper. I was also waiting for our newest potential client, and I wanted to look busy…but with anything but a computer. My once slightly too-small Schott Leather Navy Coat was, at the moment, a bit loose. A steady diet of isometric exercises, cigarettes, and whiskey over the previous few months had flattened out my usually quite round frame.

And…well, to be honest, I better

POWERBRUNCH

not tell this story. Maybe next time. Suffice it to say that it was one of those situations where I think I'm being clever and amusing (which I am…every 4th or 5th day), when maybe I'm not. My bad.

April 10

That's the date, in the year this book is being first published, that Happy Media will be celebrating its 10th Birthday. Who'd a thunk it eh?

I'm hopeful that we'll be celebrating with a combination Birthday/Book Gathering on Saturday, April 14. Ideally, we'd start here at headquarters for some snacks and to get situated and for some of us to get properly, ahem, lubricated. Next, we'd head down en masse to the Oliver Wolcott Library (www.owlibrary.org) for a quick reading (by other folks…I don't). And then, quickly the remaining 3/10 of a mile into town, and the charming 3W & Blue Bar for a tasteful feast.

But the reality of the situation is this: one of the few downside to the entirely virtual corporation is the lack of physical proximity. Let me be clear: we're more productive this way. And this maximizes our resource use efficiency (see page 1). But when you're trying to throw a party, it makes it a bigger deal than it might otherwise be.

Adam's Notes

As you've already heard me say a few times, I come from a family of journalists. As such, my creative work has always had more than a whiff of a nightly new broadcast. I present these Notes from the Desk of the Executive Director more or less as is, and not in chrono order. Some of these bits lack titles, some lack manners, and some were quite clearly written under some sort of distress. Good times....remember, I was 21 when we started this little circus.

And yet, you really can piece together something like the real story of the past 10 years in these pages.

To be honest, I feel that I spend enough time extolling the benefits of our product. And there's no question that our commitment to the community starts with me (though we could all do more). And so, at the rare times that the urge to type strikes me, I get a bit silly. I mostly like to talk about baseball, girls, golf, or everyday life. I stay out of politics and religion.

It is true that I feel quite strongly that what we've doing with Happy Media (and it has, most certainly, required the efforts of quite a few folks, C.A.L. and M.T.L. to name the two most important) is as important as any Internet Company out there. But ultimately, I'm just another wiseass who'd rather be playing roller hockey. And I think that this is just what reveals itself in my work, over and over again.

Friday, December 16, 2005

Just now, I used the ATM at the bcp bank near my home in Astoria. I was on my way to pick up the laundry. I'm out of socks. I swiped my card for entry, and proceeded to withdraw my $100. I threw out my receipt, remembered my card, and attempted to open the glass doors of the vestibule.

As it turns out, they were now magnetically sealed. Hmm. And me once again without my phone.

Luckily, I was able to flag down a passing pedestrian, and managed to give him the international symbol for "please swipe a card, any card, into the machine. So that it will let me out, as it has no right to keep me here. On a Friday evening."

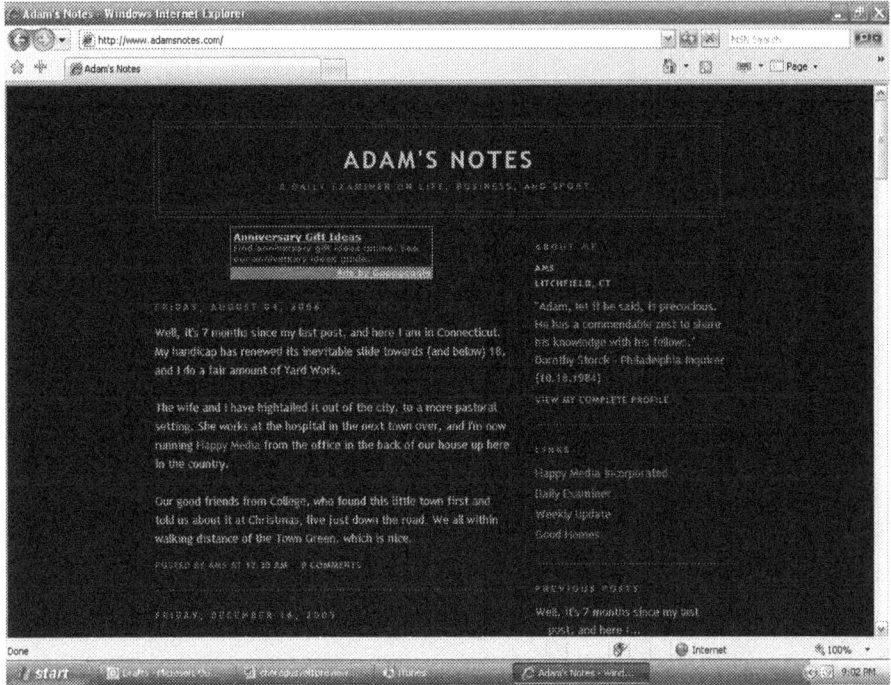

Problem solved. But really...you've got to be f****ing kidding me.

Oddly, this was the second time in 3 days that I've had problems with locked doors. The first time, however, it was entirely my own fault.

posted by ams at 6:42 PM 0 COMMENTS

There is no easy way down (Learn your craft)

As far as your dominant character traits go--arrogance glows. -
fkg

I was listening to the great Vin Scelsa's Idiot's Delight on <u>WFUV</u>
(NYC's Finest Public Radio Station) last Saturday night. As
usual, Vin played an interestingly eclectic mix of music and
interviews...everything from Uncle Floyd (remember him?) to
Hugh Masekela.

At one point in the show, after a remarkable set of 4 different,
equally moving versions of "There is no easy way down", Vin
talked with his young Engineer/Producer Kevin for a few
minutes, about the younger fellow's recent trip to Ireland. All I
can say is...kid, learn your craft. I've never heard so many
"likes" inserted into dialogue before...not even growing up in
NJ. Vin did his best to calm the youngster down, and move on
to some good radio, but the damage was already done to the
listening experience Mr. Scelsa works so hard to build and
maintain.

I remember doing the Morning Announcements for my Middle
School, back in the 80s, and being proud of how professional
we were about it, and hopefully, how entertaining. Seems like a
long time ago...and I'm sure we stunk. But pride in one's craft,

and in having a diverse skill set within it, should start very early if it's to take hold.

Hey Baby

04.08.02

I saw her face and I thought, shit, I love her. What am I going to do? The best I could do was to act indifferent, then proceed with her to the parking lot. You must never let them know that you care or they will kill you.   - Bukowski, *Hot Water Music*

We'll be taking a break for a week or two, as we do a little Spring cleaning, take care of our clients, and some necessary development on everything from Filmville's upcoming projects to Power Brunch Summit 2002.

*

On a personal level, I've always dealt better with concepts than people, with ideas rather than relationships. I'm not sure what this has to do with anything, but I'd guess it's a big part of the reason why things are the way they are. I find that this sort of thing is very much the reptilian mind competing, every second of the day, with its' more pedestrian counterpart.

*

I'm hearing whispers of another global conflict brewing...one between those intent on reducing the population of the planet to more conventionally manageable levels, and those bent on expanding our species footprint across what remains of this planet and well beyond, whatever the cost. Interesting...but not nearly enough to convince me to care too deeply about public events. When I get a moment, I'll look up that quote...

*

I highly recommend duck sauce on a toasted bagel. Avoid chasing tequila with grape jelly, stay properly hydrated, get rid of your TV, and never feel foolish for singing out loud-

09.10.2001

The internet is all about information access. If you consider yourself well-informed, and a seeker of knowledge, then there's no excuse for not being better read in the 21st Century than ever before. Every morning, I take in selected stories from the BBC, NY Daily News, CNET News, NY Post, NY Times, Washington Post, LA Times, CNN/CNNSI, ESPN, and a wide variety of other popular (and unpopular) online news sources and publications. Takes about an hour, and makes the conversation at the water cooler or meeting much more interesting.

Our ever-expanding suite of news properties provides the latest World, Internet, Finance, Entertainment, Business, Sports and DNS News, as well as original editorials, commentary and reviews from our own Network of experts. Stay tuned in the coming weeks for new designs and features throughout the Happy Media News Network.

Until next week, don't forget to remain properly hydrated-

9.10.02

One man's opinion on life, liberty, business, and baseball.

5 Disciplines

Several months ago, as some of you know, I removed the Television and PC from my living quarters. This was an effort, in part, to create an environment more conducive to mindful thought and reflection. It's been effective, to a point, but the change has also renewed my interest in Discipline (no, not that kind).

Here are a few preliminary thoughts...

1. <Fill in Yourself. What the hell do I know.>
2. Exercise: Preferably vigorous. Every day. Even for 10 minutes.
3. Respect: Give it to get it. Everyone deserves it, unless and until they prove otherwise.
4. Attire: How you look tells the world how you feel. That's right, slacker, even on Sundays.
5. Thrift: Efficient Use of Resources is not jargon...it's a better way of life.

Zen Cricket Practice

Here's what you do...get yourself a dartboard (the local pub will have one), then get good and limber. Remove all distractions from your mind (do this by listening to yourself breath and letting all thoughts, save the questions to which you're seeking answers, from your mind). Once you feel properly centered, raise your eyes and throw to a certain number on the board. Whatever the results, they reflect the overall likelihood or relative efficacy of the decision to be made. Sort of like the Magic 8-Ball...

Next Week: Going back to Jersey, Go Wildcats!

Maddening Busyness, Indeed

What a week. Happy Media continues to see a greater volume of inquiries, across the full spectrum of our service offerings. Corporate Naming seems to be having the biggest upsurge at the moment, with Internet Services and Real Estate Listings strong, as always.

I'm in the process of removing the television and pc from my place, so as to create an environment more conducive to mindfulness, and quiet reflection. The TV has been mostly unplugged for about two months anyway, but I'm still looking forward to removing it altogether.

As such, in the evenings you'll no longer experience the lightening quick responses you've come to expect. My quality of life requires it, however.

*

This girl I used to know was in a very peculiar dream I had early yesterday morning. She was in a boarding school near my old college (she was going to become a nun, I think, and seemed quite happy), and I came by for what seemed like a regular visit. Everything was pleasant and non-sinister. Then some woman wouldn't let me leave the school grounds, because my driver's license had expired. F*cking weird...

I mentioned this dream to a female friend about an hour ago. She said something rude about a genetic predisposition towards madness, and suggested that the girl might be a phantom, or a figment. Oh well...

Letter

From: ~(UltraDense)~ [mailto:nix6_9@yahoo.com]
Sent: Sunday, May 22, 2005 8:53 PM
To: newsletter@weeklyupdate.com
Subject: where's Adam?

I'm a first time writer long time reader and I think that the newsletter is lacking the personal draw that used to come from Adam's notes. I think i speak for the majority of the weekly update readers that we are hungry for adams insights into corporate america, life and baseball. I know Mr. Sherwin is busy with his new wife. but we the reading public beseech you for more input lest we bite toungues for wont of meal to fill our minds and our souls or maybe just for another outlet of someones bullshit!

First Hacks of Spring - *03/02/02*

1:30 PM - I've attempted to make my way to the cage for my first taste of mechanical pitching since October, only to be waylaid by the fact that our Telecommunications Provider has switched, leaving Happy Media Headquarters without it's popular Reverse Lateral Voicemail Scheme.

1:58 PM - Once again saved by Operations, I'm on my way. As usual I've arrived somewhat later than most to camp, but I believe my strenuous off-season conditioning program will leave me set for a break-out year.

2:16 PM - I've returned to the office, having made an appointment for 15 minutes with the Pitching Machine of my choice at 4:15. I plan to start with 10 minutes on 80 MPH, and then either 5 more on 80, or if I'm feeling up to it, the final 5 on 90.

4:57 PM - Spring Training has finally begun for young adam. Not bad, considering the nearly 4-month layoff...I'm hitting the ball hard, and my always cranky right shoulder seems fine thus far. I'm still pulling the ball a bit too much, and uncharacteristically, I popped up a few bunts, but now I'm home, having picked up the laundry on my way, and need a good shower.

Early Season Slumps

04.22.02

Mean nothing. Like Joe said the other day, "the 2002 Yankees will be evaluated at the end of the year. Not now."

Context

It seems that it's what most people are looking for...and context within which to live their lives enjoyably and comfortably, and still function as normal citizens of some sort or another. For me it's Happy Media. Whether I'm writing, teaching, making movies, or staring slack jawed out the window...I have a specific filter I can apply that will give me creative freedom, commercial opportunity, and whatever else I need.

Apparently

- I was always this way (oddly reassuring)
- people who knew you when you were 11 have a distinct advantage
- email often allows for great misunderstanding, especially of tone
- admit it...you liked it

Trim The Fat

Like a warped, ongoing version of the Freshman 15, Happy Media's first 5 years gave its co-founder about 10 pounds per. Half of that has been sweated out in the past 8 weeks, with another 25 scheduled for exorcism in the next 8. So if Young

Adam snarls at you, or behaves even more strangely than usual, its not his being raised wrong...its dehydration.

And you know what I always say, ladies and gentlemen...say it with me...it's important to remain properly hydrated. Just keep your hands and feet away from his mouth, and slowly back away from the cage.

Another Summer

The more time you put into something, the better stuff you can make. So, what I do is, I work seven days a week. I don't take vacations. Never have, actually. So I can put in more time.   - Gene Simmons

It's the end of June again, so that means PC Expo (now TechXNY) at the Javitz Center. I'm not a big fan of trade shows. We Happy Media folk mostly prefer to get some work done. That said, part of our Mission is to disseminate information, so we're always happy to have an opportunity to let you know what's going on in the various industries associated with this and other events.

I do remember my first such working event. 1992 found a 16 year old running the DDC Publishing booth, at a far more crowded show than this is likely to be. We sold a few books, lost a few pounds in sweat carrying them across town, and failed to enjoy the warehouse ambiance in the lower level of the Convention Center.

On the Horizon

This weekend will mark the beginning of our Annual Summer Rebuild, as all of the Happy 100 gets a total or partial overhaul and tune-up. We've got some talented new outsourced professionals working with us, as well as our always extensive database of pre-worn developers and in-house talent, so be ready for some robust and interesting productivity.

Don't Do That

My principal anguish and the source of all my joys and sorrows from my youth onward has been the incessant, merciless battle between the spirit and the flesh. - **Nikos Kazantzakis**

Everybody needs a bosom for a pillow. Everybody needs a bosom. Mine's on the forty-five -**Cornershop**

I can't believe it, the way you look sometimes. Like a trampled flag on a city street. -**Bad Religion**

I've recently found it difficult to keep a clear perspective on many things. Running this sort of company, one that's involved in everything from <u>Movie Making</u> to <u>Outsource Management</u>, is enough of a mindfuck. When you factor in the precisely unusual manner in which we've gone about building this little slice of pie, its not difficult to imagine how Young Sherwin might get a bit out of sorts.

Moreso than usual, I've been attempting a deliberate mindfulness about matters personal and professional. It only seems logical to treat each instance individually, all very Vipassana and all, when one experiences from hour to hour, note to note, are so varied, good and bad. Ptl-

*

When i was 11, at sleepaway summer camp in the catskills, i had my first girlfriend. she was 9, and her name was *****. she was a nice girl from brooklyn. it was a strange little thing, as all these things are (especially at that age).

The strangest thing about it was that her best friend, also named *****, i liked better. who can say why, or what, but it was so. she was a tiny little redhead with a slightly bad attitude...very smart.

I came across the name of the second ***** in some ***** law school stuff. she's in her last weeks in law school....as...wait for it.....a public policy lawyer (or at least her name was in a public policy journal). couldn't help it, and emailed her, inquiring whether was the same. Much hilarity and deserved abuse have ensued.

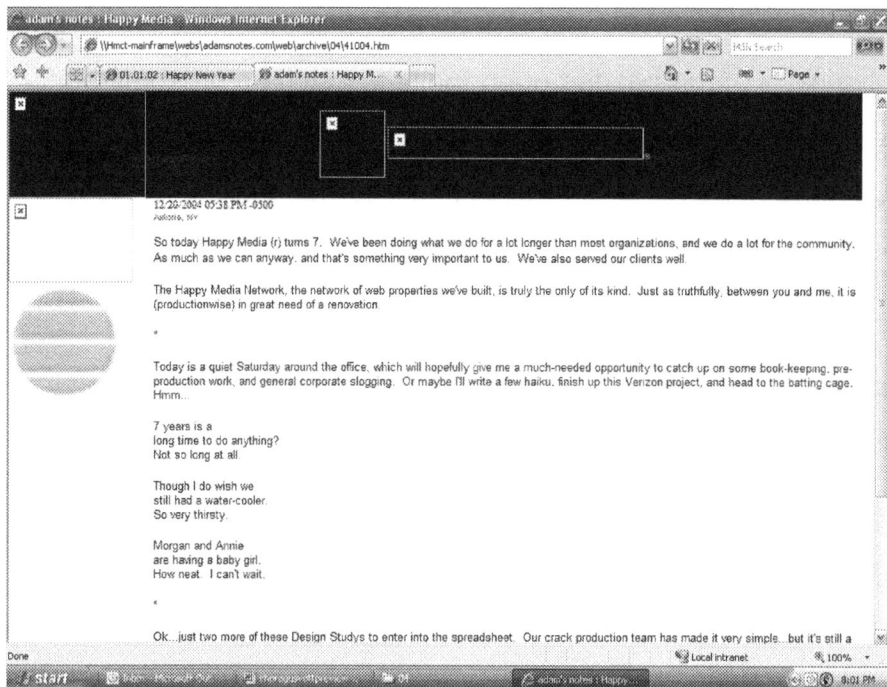

12/20/2004 05:38 PM -0500
Astoria, NY

So today Happy Media (r) turns 7. We've been doing what we do for a lot longer than most organizations, and we do a lot for the community. As much as we can anyway, and that's something very important to us. We've also served our clients well.

The Happy Media Network, the network of web properties we've built, is truly the only of its kind. Just as truthfully, between you and me, it is (productionwise) in great need of a renovation.

*

Today is a quiet Saturday around the office, which will hopefully give me a much-needed opportunity to catch up on some book-keeping, pre-production work, and general corporate slogging. Or maybe I'll write a few haiku, finish up this Verizon project, and head to the batting cage. Hmm...

7 years is a
long time to do anything?
Not so long at all.

Though I do wish we
still had a water-cooler.
So very thirsty.

Morgan and Annie
are having a baby girl.
How neat. I can't wait.

*

Ok...just two more of these Design Studys to enter into the spreadsheet. Our crack production team has made it very simple...but it's still a pain in the ass. I remember doing similar work for CIBC Oppenheimer, Paine-Webber, Citibank, and a bunch of others...mostly as a temp.

*

Well, it's a lovely day out. Unseasonably cool and very bright and sunny. I've done most of what I came here this morning to do, so I'm getting out of there for now. Home to shower, then to the batting cage for some much-needed work and then, oddly, to the gym.

ams
11:32 AM

Today

9.02.03

It's just 1 PM, and it's already been a productive day. I've made/received about a dozen human resources and bizdev phone calls, sent out and received a bunch of emails for similar purposes, finished two proposals and some client webwork, been to the bank, gotten a haircut, dropped off my laundry, and we're about to send out this here newsletter.

This follows an impressive bit of housecleaning yesterday, which involved about a dozen garbage bags of, well, garbage being removed from my apartment. I've decided to try to live as a bit less of a savage for a little while, and I'm even giving some consideration to doing some grocery shopping and/or sweeping/mopping.

I hope everyone had a pleasant holiday. It's 59 degrees out, cold and dark here in Astoria. Nearly Autumnal. I like it-

ams

Siam
(2.26.03, Astoria, NY)

Well, where to begin? This was a voyage of new personal highs for this still proudly provincial Jersey boy.

Longest Travel by Plane (Multiple Flights): 21 Hours, JFK to Anrchorage to Taipei to Bangkok)
Longest Travel by Plane (Single Flight): 16 Hours, Taipei to JFK
Longest Travel by Train: 15 Hours, Bangkok to Trang
Longest Travel by Bus: 12 Hours, Krabi to Bangkok

I highly recommend the beach at Ton Sai (just West of Rai Lai, near Au Nang), which has both excellent rock climbing and BASE Jumping (and no, you'll never see me doing either one). I'm also grateful for the sartorial expertise of King's Intl. Tailor, down at the end of Khao Sanh road in Bangkok. Ask for Andrew.

I nearly didn't make my plane back from Bangkok Tuesday morning, due to having come down with some sort of severe illness the night before. I arrived in NYC last night, and am still quite ill. And, as usual whenever I'm under the weather, Team Happy Media has a beacoup big meeting tomorrow...

(2.10.03, Astoria, NY)

Roughly 36

Hours until I head 10,000 miles West, to go to the East. I stay out of politics, but read up on the good work being done at <u>Dr. Cynthia's Mae Tao Clinic</u>.

Hmm...

Here's an interesting story from today's <u>NY Times</u>. Continuing a trend, the Gray Lady talks about how some companies are taking a new (um...or actually an old) approach to marketing their products and services online. This groundbreaking piece echoes what we have been saying for quite a few years now. Luckily, we practice what we preach, and have built our network according to the fundamental business principles we jabber about so relentlessly.

Provincial

Jersey boy that I am, I have never so much as owned a passport prior to this past week. So naturally I'm eager, despite the remarkably poor timing, to venture forth for some much needed rest. I will, however, have access to email even while in my bungalow at the beach, so do keep in touch.

The Movies

...not many directors can be bothered to approach what is still the most taxing of dramatic subjects. Forget superheroes, or the reëmergence of wizards with beards down to their belts; try filming the tale of an ordinary man. It is the topic of a demotic age, and film still doesn't know what to make of it. - ANTHONY LANE, The New Yorker

We're couldn't agree more. And this is what we'll be looking to do when we (hopefully this July) begin production on Happy Media's first Filmville Production. Stay tuned for more info about this most favored of my many pets.

Media Business Outlook '03 (Intro)

I've been writing (with, I dare say, some measurable prescience) about Media in general (and New Media specifically) since the mid-80's. First at the NY Daily News, then at a wide variety of Consumer and Trade publications. I am not, however, wholly unbiased as to the future of these various inter-related industries. I believe that the methods we've used to build our Network are those necessary to create a strong, sustainable enterprise that provides superior value to its clients, users, corporate partners, and staff, while benefiting the community. Harrumph and so on.

In advance of my looking ahead to '03, here's some of what I said about 2002:

Tripping

12.08.03, 8:23 AM

Three weeks ago New Hampshire, two weeks ago Massachusetts, this past snowy weekend Maryland, this coming weekend Florida...wow. I tend to stay right here an Astoria for months at a time, but this season seems to be a significant exception to that rule. I suspect that the New Year will find me here at home more regularly...so for all those folks right here at home I haven't seen lately...you're welcome.

Lighters and Shades

Seem to disappear from my possession with remarkable rapidity. I've gone through at least 2 of each in the last week or two. Which, I suppose, may very well be related to that first item.

Irony As a Value

Passenger: I don't know....he's very...
Driver: Texan?
Passenger: Yeah...he's very Texan.
Driver: Nothing wrong with that. At least those people have values. As opposed to up here, where irony passes for a value.

Razorfish

Surprising no one, the name and organization that to many represented the heights (but more accurately, the lows) of the late 90's Internet Business silliness, Razorfish, will cease to exist (see article here). Simply stated, these clowns (though the founders in question left the firm some time ago) for a time gave anyone looking to build a lasting New Media business a bad name. Happy Media®, however, is still here. We have our issues to address, but we continue to build, serve, and innovate. Sadly, however, we still lack a wall-through fish tank.

Pneumonia

An album I have been playing again and again lately (downloaded version, naturally) was recently being played by the couple in the apartment with which I share a bedroom wall. As I have a bad habit (one of many) of playing a few songs I like over and over until they lose their grip on my brain (megalomania), it was peculiar to barely hear the songs running through their natural course, without any action taken on my part. Despite the thin walls, it was mostly the bass that allowed me to recognize, and then identify, what I was hearing. I continue to think about this, but I have no idea why, or what it might mean. Especially since my fever at the time (a robust but not dangerous 102) likely imbued the hour or so with greater significance then it would have merited otherwise. Tomorrow, I return to my brusque, shiny-headed MD for more aggressive treatment, as I still sound like a consumptive after two weeks.

The Subtext

I suspect, that despite being a fairly perceptive fellow (with regards to business and sport), that a great deal of the time I have absolutely no idea what many of the people in my life are talking about. What they really mean. I also suspect, however, that this is the case for most of us.

Coming Soon: IBS (Irritable B*stard Syndrome), More Epigraphs and Epigrams

10/08/02

There is nothing so captivating to a young woman as her own reflection. -ams

This girl I know...every email I get from her, the clock is always waaay off. Reminds me of what I used to do with my alarm clock, back when I had a real job, so as to trick my sorry ass into getting up earlier. Now of course, I'm usually in the office early, even on the weekends, like some sort of geriatric insomniac.

———

Nothing I enjoy more than a challenge...my confidence is matched only by my belief that occasional failure is indicative of a healthy effort to test one's ability. Although, I do prefer situations where I believe that I have at least some influence over the outcome.

———

I do believe that the less time I have to spend in places like that one last night, the longer I will live. That entire neighborhood is sullen, with snarky bartenders and lousy music.

———

Most of the time these days, you'll find me in a suit. But I find that the more I start the dress like the "villain" in the "coming of age" movie, the more often I get to behave/act like the hero. You know...nice.

———

Less Fat, More Bastard

Years of telemarketing have left me unwilling to pick up a phone unless its ringing. I type fast, and have much to say (or think so), so these three factors combine to have Young Sherwin sending out a great deal of email. This sometimes leads to misunderstandings with people who don't know me all that well, or who aren't familiar with my peculiarly ineffective "verbal stream-of-consciousness"* style.

Waxing poetic for the last few weeks has been a pleasant distraction, but now it's time to get back down to business. Some of our beloved clients out there, and you know who you are, have been taking advantage of this rare disorganized period of time. Alas, my dear friends, I'm back. So expect things to change...other than our providing you with superior value.

I was

Looking at some of the writing I had done when I was an actual adolescent (rather than a perpetual one). Stuff for the Daily News, for other newspapers, creative stuff, trade magazine stuff, etc. Wow...not good. Except for some of the more creative pieces, and some work I did in High School. It's no wonder my Notes are so damn limited, under the circumstances.

Mawwaige

10.31.03, 9:02 AM

Two weeks ago, at the opening of APAC's new season, I slipped a small fabric box into the hand of My Nurse, as we settled in to watch the rest of the show (she arrived late, having driven down from New Hampshire). She gave me a curious look.

She opened the box, saw that there was a ring inside, and slipped it on her finger. Showing remarkable poise and composure, she smiled and took my hand, and then we watched, or pretended to watch, the last 5 minutes until the intermission, then went outside. Being the smart, sassy, well-educated (Mt. Holyoke, Columbia) girl that she is, she said no. Just kidding. Actually, we went to Cafe Brick for a much-needed drink, and that was that...

The reactions we've received have ranged from "wha?" to "Holy Shit! Are you kidding?". While everyone was happy for us, once convinced that I wasn't kidding, my friends and parents in particular were highly skeptical that I had actually done this. June 5th is the date, and it'll be taking place here. More on this soon...

The Clothes Make the Man (I Didn't Recognize You)

> how would you know. you did not even graduate from high
> school. - fkg

I speak often with our Acting President about the duality of life. Especially Happy Media life. And somehow, I think this is expressed most fully by a certain phenomenon I've noticed here in my neighborhood: When I open up the office in the morning, or head to the batting cage in the evening, I'm usually in ripped sweatpants, a hoody of some sort, and a backwards yankee hat. The rest of the time, I'm usually in a suit or equivalent. I sometimes see the same people, 5 minutes apart, and they do not recognize me. If I wind up actually conversing with them, they tell me so.

Taking Out The Garbage

That's right...I take it out. Especially when we're having one of those remarkably production and/or frustrating days/weeks that I'm pretty sure only happen here, it's a great way to clear the head. Like a shot of bourbon without the sour stomach. I highly recommend it for all biz types who are wishing they were back in their younger years, washing dishes somewhere. It has helped ease my evolution from ne'er do well dirtbag to corporate swine.

Take It Where You Can Get It

May your fondest wish be granted. - Traditional Chinese curse

I've had a perfectly wonderful evening. But this wasn't it. - Groucho Marx

A little inaccuracy sometimes saves tons of explanation. - H. H. Munro (Saki)

What a strange illusion it is to suppose that beauty is goodness. - Leo Tolstoy

So I'm sitting in the window of my living room last night, smoking a rare cigarette. The garbage bags have been stacked beside the tree at the curb, along with an old filing cabinet, and a mattress. A rather disheveled looking Gentleman walks (or staggers) by, takes one look at the twin-sized rubber pad, dives onto it, and immediately achieves a comatose state that my usually sleepless self could not hope to emulate. Last time I looked, he was still there...

Socks, T-Shirts, and Underwear

For some reason, I never have enough of them. And far too often, I find myself wearing garments in serious need of some mending. One of these days, I'll get around to stocking up...

40/40/40

As of press time, Mr. Soriano remains one jack short of that exclusive club (hr/doubles/sb). Along with the return of The Sandman, what must embolden the always robust pinstriped postseason outlook is the way, in the past few weeks, the kid has been going with the pitch, and not lunging at the mushy breaking stuff they usually throw him.

Some Unrelated Truths and other Observations
New York, NY: 03.25.02

- People only read/hear half of what you write or say

- In my case, and some others, that's often a good thing

- Efficient use of resources and diversity of revenue streams will build a strong business

- You all hate when I mix business with my customary babbling

- Nothing is quite so distracting to a young woman as her own reflection

- Singing out loud is pretty fucking good for you

- So is spooning

- And turning on a 90 MPH fastball

- Don't forget nougat

Spring has arrived, so let's here it loud....**God Bless America and Yankee Baseball**.

I'd like to say a few things about the written word. I know, we're making movies these days, but in the end, it all comes down to the language arts.

I've had some discussions lately, amongst folks more educated that I prefer, about what constitutes, in these dissolute times, Serious Literature. Here's the thing...if the prose comes from someplace real in the author's head, from some aspect of the interior monologue, it's serving the most essential purpose of all the arts: communication. Any writing that does this, or makes an honest pass at it, is a serious work. Any work that does not attempt to communicate in that fashion might as well be an Air Conditioner User Manual or Serial Science Fiction.

More later, hopefully with some greater frame of reference-

A Look Back (Oh Dear)
(1.01.03, Astoria, NY)

Here are some recently unearthed NY Daily News clips of mine from the mid-to-late 80's (ladies, please note the devilish look, and the tie and coat on Very Young Adam). As any of you who read this column are well aware, my best typing days are behind me. Fortunately, this archival stuff is not my best of that decade, and thus is less clear evidence of that fact.

12.28.86 (For the record: I was never a computer nut)
01.11.87 (Page 15 of the NY Life section. Page 16? Ann Landers on why "Talk is Chic, Sex is Nix On First Date Even Today)
12.03.89 (Floppy New Year, Indeed)

Tip of the cap, and unlimited mini-golf privileges to Herr Director, The Families, The Kid, The Acting President, Ms. Wong and the entire StaffWire and Entry Draft teams for their stellar work this year. Nods are also due to, in no particular order, Madame Sosostris, Dorothy, Ms. Steiner, The Old Man & Sideshow, JoMamma, Lois Lane, My Nurse, The Admiral, and many others for giving me something to write about. Most of these folks are even speaking to me at the moment, so it must have been a good year. Best wishes to everyone here, and those I have momentarily neglected to mention, for a Happy, Healthy, Creative, and Prosperous '03.

You Tell'em, Cash

"The typical whining that's going on in baseball about the Yankees needs to stop. We pay a lot of money in revenue sharing and the luxury tax. We're about winning. If these other teams choose not to spend their money on players, that's their problem." Brian Cashman

Just 44 Days until Pitchers and Catchers report.

Birth, Death, Taxes

New York, NY : 09.12.01

Thousands of people died suddenly yesterday. It's impossible to over or under state that fact. It just is.

Thousands of people were also born yesterday. Maybe not in this scarred, burning city, but not far. People to whom this *thing* will seem hopelessly distant...who will have no understanding of **before this**.

In the life in between, there is a great deal of simple pain and joy, enthusiasm and apathy, ignorance and... every once in a while, one of us comes closer to enlightenment. To knowing better.

I can tell you this: look to your left, look to your right, then look at yourself...it's not any of us.

Growing up a 3rd-Generation *news person,* I've long-since had the detached technique down pat. The magnitude of this thing changes everything. It goes beyond usually indomitable spirit of cynicism that we have developed.

Today, there is great loss of life, our liberty has suffered, no business is being done and no baseball is being played.

The Kid Can Play

New York, NY : 10.16.01

Once again, amid cries of Big Media Market advantages, home-grown Yankees take the team where it needs to go. Derek Jeter, Mariano Rivera, Alfonso Soriano, Ramiro Mendoza, along with an assortment of other players mostly acquired in reasonable trades, saw the wheels come off of the Oakland Athletics talented young team, and once again did not fail to capitalize.

Now it's on to Seattle, for a showdown between the last run of this Yankee team as we know it, with the Mariner crew that beat the '98 Yankees record regular season with a 116-win juggernaut.

Don't Look Now

Just as the wide range of Happy Media properties has appeared to reach maximum density, we're about to put together some projects, with a few corporate partners, that will dramatically impact the way people think about New Media Business in the Year 2001. Stay tuned for more Joint efforts between Happy Media and Grand Concourse Media, as well as new versions of Silicon Realtor and Promodome.

Sweet Child of Mine

(3.14.03, Astoria, NY)

I find that, like a good belt of whiskey, it does the trick nearly every time. Gets the blood flowing, without artificial chemicals, and the effects usually last at least a bit longer than Axl's warble. Then again, there is great wisdom to be received from the words and music of Ronny Van Zant, may he rest in peace. Between Simple Man, Tuesday's Gone, That Smell, and Freebird...it's all there. Life lessons, from a man who didn't know how to ski, and who died too damn young.

Editorializing

I've been accused of it yet again, by the always delightfully willful Ms. Maddy. Here are the two primary definitions:

- To express an opinion in or as if in an editorial.

- To present an opinion in the guise of an objective report.

In the particular instance in question, I proudly proclaim my innocence. Though as a rule, most would agree that I'm guilty as charged. Thankfully, it remains amongst the least objectionable of my bad habits. See? Not even a single Happy Days joke. What a good boy I am...

Blurry, Indeed

(Astoria, NY, 5.17.03)

When I returned to NYC in mid-December of '95, I was coming off of a very strange year. New Year's day of '95 had seen me ruining my mattress, in a newly rented apartment not far from Boston's Symphony Hall.

I spent 5 months in Beantown, working primarily as a temp, salesman, and telemarketer. I wandered near-penniless through the streets of that lovely city, often waking in the middle of the night to walk and sit by an enormous reflecting pool not far from my apartment. Not knowing anyone but my friend and roommate, and his girlfriend, I enjoyed the anonymity.

One of the few contacts I had with my previous life was a female classmate of mine from High School who was attending Harvard. I don't remember how we ran into one another, but she dropped by the apartment one day unannounced, as I was mid bong-hit. I screamed like a little girl in surprise as she walked through the door. Once I calmed down, I mentioned that I had just quit my job. She wouldn't believe me, insisting that it was OK...I could tell her that had been fired.

Still Running

New York, NY : 09.24.01

Despite recent events, the Happy Media train keeps on running. We've recently launched new versions of <u>Weekly Update</u>, <u>Daily Examiner</u>, and several other key sites. Keep an eye out in the coming weeks for additional <u>Directory</u> projects, as well as a few New Ventures. In some cases, The Network is headed into directions that would have been unthinkable just a year or two ago.

We're still working on some of the more code intensive aspects of our <u>Membership</u> package, so stay tuned for more info about our <u>Admin Panel</u>, and other features Under Development. Included in our Free Membership is a subscription to Weekly Update, as well as an across the board 10% discount on all of our already competitively priced services.

Back to Work

New York, NY : 09.18.01

We Happy Media folks do our best not to take ourselves too seriously. We're very serious about our work, while remaining aware of the fact that business is important, but not life and death. This past week has been a firm reminder of that.

Yes, our beloved Yankees go back to work today. Yes, The Happy Media Network is operating at full capacity. But somehow, it all seems to be tempered with a certain awareness.

Well, enough of that...our services and products are still the best value around. So by all means, order a Web Site, purchase a Domain Name, let us build your Animated Movie or perform your Market Research. And, at the very least, give your time or money to the organizations below.

Today, business is being done and baseball is being played.

Go Wildcats!

9.17.02

I remember the Autumn I spent covering State Championship Lee High School Football for The Berkshire Record. I was about High School age at the time (17), but I was away at a weird little college in Western Mass. I had a great time covering the games and writing my column (and doing the stats for the Radio broadcasts). This was some of my best writing, and I got my first peek into small town politics, but this was the season that I figured out that I didn't want to write for a living. At least not in that fashion. More on this topic later...

Next Week: Socks, T-Shirts, and Underwear

Autumn Manifesto
9.23.03

The 2003 autumnal equinox occurred at 4:47 a.m. this morning in the Northern Hemisphere. As a rule these past 6 or 7 years (the length of time HMI has been around), this season is the one most usually marked by a significant upswing in my productivity. This is probably due to the fact that I prefer cooler weather, the Yankees have been mostly playing well, and Autumn in New York is ideal for someone like me. To that end, here's a Personal Productivity Checklist for the next few months, while I work on finishing this essay:

-less loitering
-write/publish/exercise every day
-fewer cigarettes
-improve record-keeping here at HMI

I've gotten a head start on most of these things, but we'll see how it goes. Stay tuned for some new creative work, and updated/edited versions of some of the older stuff...

Media Biz '03 Cont'd

(1.27.03, Astoria, NY)

I think we'll begin to see a refocusing of some of the major media businesses back towards the Media itself. A company in these related industries must, in the final analysis, produce content of interest in order to remain a sustainable enterprise. It's not just enough, with all the new outlets the public has for information and entertainment, to throw any old product up there, and focus exclusively on selling advertising. Also, I think we'll be looking at more than a few traditionally product/info Media Enterprises shift some of their excess internal and outsourced production capability towards outside client service provision.

Talking to Oneself

It's often hard to tell these days which people are actually talking to themselves, and which are yapping away on those cell phone attachments. I'm perhaps more inclined to assume the former than I should be, but the later I find to be just as much of a sign of madness. Having become quite the techno-phobe, I don't talk on the phone when I can avoid it, and would never use one of those hands-free sets. That way at least I know when I'M talking to myself.

In Medias Res

3.19.03

is without question a favorite literary technique of mine. I don't like to spin my wheels if it can be avoided. It's also the title of a new work of mine, which appears to be evolving out of some of the other things I've been toying with over the past year or so. Those of you unbusy enough to be reading these notes on a semi-regular basis should get a sneak peek in a month or so.

Politics and Religion

are the two things that I studiously avoid talking about, in this space or any other. Let's just say that I like to focus on providing superior value to our clients, and other business related matters. That having been said, my cousin Davy, who's still in the Navy, and probably will be for life...deserves a tip of the cap.

Trying Our Luck

I just can't help but wonder what has happened to that dangerously disarming, oddly illusive old friend of mine. Oh dear...must've been something I said.

Sketches of Spain

New York, NY: 12.14.01

Due to the looming darkness, cold and dampness, and the Annual December Client Coma, I had an opportunity to listen again to this fine piece of music late this afternoon. I know nothing about jazz, and like little of it, but this album has stayed with me since I first heard it's opening notes as a teenager. Turn off the damn TV, go buy/borrow/steal this thing, turn off all the lights, and light some candles or incense. You're welcome.

Rip Torn, on Miles Davis, from <u>Esquire Magazine</u>:

I used to be friends with Miles Davis. He didn't like many folks. I lived across the street from him. He would call me up sometimes—"I got some fish I wanna cook up for ya." I went up there, and he was on a couch, looking out the window. He was just rapt. I said, "What're you watching, Miles?" He said, "The traffic. Where are all these motherfuckers goin'?"

Unfinished
Works

I've always been fascinated with works in progress. Anything that appears to give you a peek at something you're not really supposed to see. Like the sort of thing you'd be likely to find in the back of a volume of stuff, recently recovered, from someone long dead.

That's pretty much what we have here. A bunch of stuff that I loaded a great deal of creative output into, then was unable to finish, due to time, inclination, or the constant psychic demand running a business can extract.

From the time I was about 7, until a year or two ago, I was almost certain that typing for a living was, one way or another, going to be my fate. My Grandfather had been, as I discussed earlier, a newspaperman for many years, and my father had followed in his footsteps after his early, untimely death. I had first written for the NY Daily News as a pre-teen, and The Berkshire Record as a 17 year old covering State Championship football. *Go wildcats!*

Like my notes in the previous section, these works are presented more or less as-is, without polishing or delousing.

Incogni Comics

Incogni Comics was, for me, one of the more exciting projects we worked on in the past 10 years. This is even though it ultimately has gone nowhere (for the time being). The entire creation process, for perhaps for the first time, took place with little or no input from me, except at a strictly casual level. On the next page are the character-level results that I could find with a preliminary search of our archives. There are several more. Emmanuel Bryan, who was originally an Entry Draft intern, did the artwork, under the supervision and direction of Matt LaRose, Happy Media's Director of Operations. I contributed exactly one thing…the approximate verbal sketch of the red-headed girl.

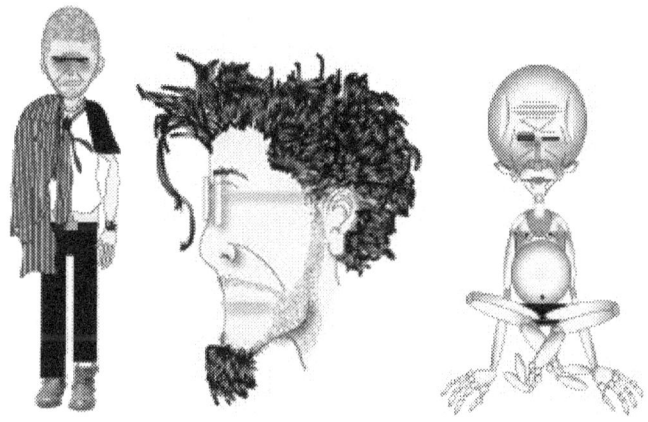

The Hardest Part

(a short film)

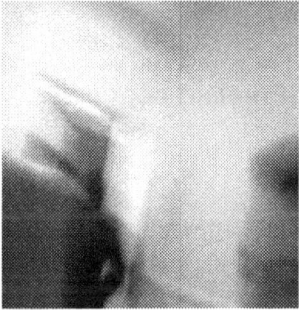

June:

Dark hair, Long Island/NJ semi-trash but reasonably well-educated and dressed. Crooked but well-meaning family, cold but kind hacker friends. Sometimes tactless, hotheaded, and slightly out of touch with reality. Not entirely certain she's doing the right thing, but determined to never let this be visible to the others or interfere with her decision making process.

Will (Wilson):

Trustafarian. Uptight, paranoid, not as smart but slightly more socially able than the girls. The sort of guy most everyone likes, but people often don't remember his name. He stays out of situations requiring too much critical thinking, but is educated enough to sometimes give the impression of feeling superior.

Mo (Maureen):

Distant, unavailable hacker. Unconventionally attractive, grumpy, possibly unwell in some serious way. Calls Will "Wilson." Thinks that people don't know that she'd rather be more animated, more off the cuff, and less introspective. Is also determined not to allow this introspection to interfere with how she makes important decisions, and the life she has planned out for herself.

Secondary:

Three people (2 men, 1 woman) smoking on landing in between roof and office scenes. Must be willing to make the most out of a few lines. Will have some limited dialogue flexibility. The people in them (and we may need more) need to be distinct.

Voiceovers:

Female - Petulant, bored, and crisp

Male – Earnest and nervous

Scenes:

- a "natural movie", no postproduction magic...just well edited, with nice fades. part documentary, part music video

- Two girls are cheating Will of his "Trustifarian" account?

- Credits, 1 minute front and back

1. Roof #1, Will and June, "we need to be there...", "cigarette",

"freefall", 4 minutes

2. Roof to Office, in between scene #1, "american jesus", 1 minute

3. Office #1, Mo, June, Will, "volleyball, famous dead people", 5 minutes

4. Office to roof, In between Scene #2, Captain Mike, 1 minute

5. 4 minutes

6. Roof to Office, In between scene #3, "Smoking, montage and voiceover", 2 minutes

7. Roof, Cut back to ding and envelope, 4 minutes

Setting:

ams office (lava lamp), hallway, stairwell, roof

Characters:

June – Dark hair, Long Island/NJ but well-educated, well-dressed and classy. Mob family, hacker friends. Sometimes tactless, hotheaded, and slightly out of touch with reality in a "let them eat cake" sort of way.

Will – (Wilson) Trustafarian. Uptight, paranoid, not as smart but more socially able than the girls. The sort of guy everyone likes, but people often don't remember his last name.

Moe – (Maureen Joan "mojo") Distant, blonde hacker. Unconventionally attractive, grumpy. Calls Will "Wilson."

Secondary: three people (undetermined) smoking on landing in between roof and office scenes.

actions and general directions:

1 trip to roof (dusk), many cigarettes, periodical typing and mousing, 1 slap, two phonecalls (1 outgoing, 1 incoming)

quick cuts, constant and increasing beats and music

Suggested Soundtrack to "The Hardest Part":

Eleanor Rigby (Godhead): 3:43

American Jesus (Bad Religion): 3:16

Psycho Killer (Talking Heads - live): 4:35

Me Gustas Tu (Manu Chao): 3:59

Bleed American (Jimmy Eat World): 3:01

Exit Music (for a film) (Radiohead): 4:26

music:

for each change, we see winamp

Scene 1: The Roof

June and Will. Will is pacing, June is smoking a cigarette, staring out at the NYC skyline (which never pans and only shows the Empire State Building shot, above the ex-WTC)

Will: (pacing, neurotic, paranoid) Why are we out here?

June: (drags on cigarette) I needed a cigarette.

Will: We need to be there. We need to be there when it happens.

June: (takes very long drag on cigarette, lets it out slowly) Its not going to happen for another three hours.

Will: What if it happens early? I'm going back downstairs.

June: (ashes) 'Kay.

Will: (walks towards stairwell, stops, comes back) You're sure its going to be three hours?

June: Hmmm?

Will: I mean, that's what she told you, right? She said its going to be three hours?

June: (takes last long puff on cigarette) No, what she said was that you should invest in yoga classes so you don't get such a stiff neck when you blow yourself. (crushes out cigarette) I said its going to be three hours.

Will: Give me a cigarette.

June hands him one. He lights up, puffs once and looks at the cigarette in disgust.

Will: God. How can you smoke these fucking things?

June: I like them that way. They build character.

Will (sensing an opportunity): God knows you could use some of that.

Will puffs one more time, puts out cigarette, rolls it between his fingers, staring at it. Senses silence...

Will: (conversationally) Did you know that it takes 9.4 seconds for a body, any body, to reach terminal velocity when released from 20,000 feet above sea level.

June: (vaguely) No.

Will: If you dive out of a plane, and your shoots fail at ten thousand feet, that leaves eight whole seconds before you hit the ground.

June: (uninterested) Really?

Will: That must be the longest fucking eight seconds in the world. Eight whole seconds with nothing to do but think, I'm gonna die now.

Will reaches for another cigarette from the pack on the ledge, but the girl snatches it back in annoyance.

Will: Longest eight seconds in the whole fucking world. Don't you think?

June: (petulantly) I'm going in.

Will stares at cigarette, still rolling it between his fingers. He looks down and drops it off the roof. Shot of cigarette falling in slow motion and, perhaps, hitting the ground.

Scene 2: The Office

Second Girl (Mo) is sitting at computer. Will is lying on couch throwing volleyball against the wall and catching it. June (from roof) is sitting on desk with back against the wall reading last few pages of very large book.

Ds, fade in

interior, ams office, tripod shot from on top of desk, at angle facing couch/window

June: (sweating, wiping forehead) Christ it's hot in here. Can't you do something about...

Mo: The AC is on full-blast...just wait for it to take effect. And stop fanning yourself, you know that only makes it worse.

Will: (tosses volleyball) Has it come yet?

Mo: No.

Will: (gets up excitedly and points at little envelope) What's that?

Mo: An e-mail from my uncle Ed.

Will: (lies back down and throws ball up in the air halfheartedly) Oh.

June: (slams book down) God this was such crap! Crap, I tell you!

Will: (ignoring June) How's Uncle Ed?

Mo: Divorced. Crabby. Probably gay.

June: I can't believe I read the entire book! Crap!

Will: (tosses ball against wall again) Oh.

Mo: He's trying to set up some gambling thing in Burkina Faso.

June: I've just wasted whole hours of my life.

Will: (tosses ball at ceiling) Burkina Faso?

Mo: Its in Africa.

June: I'll never get that time back! Doesn't anyone care?

Silence. Will tosses volleyball at wall next to window. It misses and sails out open window.

Will: (mildly) Shit.

Mo: (turns from computer) What?

June: (slightly hysterical) Are you insane!? You could kill someone like that! We could get sued!

They assemble at the window. Possible shot from outside of all three looking out.

Mo: Do you see it?

June: No. It probably bounced over to the next street and killed some old lady crossing the street!

Will: (mournfully) I lost my volleyball.

Famous Dead People

Moe: Biggie Smalls.

June: Who?

Moe: The Notorious B.I.G.

Will: He's dead?

Moe: Yes.

Will: Tupac Shakur.

June: Ehhh... ummm... John Lennon.

Moe: Fair enough... Roger Maris.

Will: Napoleon Bonaparte.

June: Vasco Da Gama.

Moe: Jacques Cousteau.

Will: Franz Ferdinand.

June: Dwight David Eisenhower.

Moe: Mamie Eisenhower.

Will: Easy-E.

June: Why are you doing this? I don't know any rap people. Umm... Sirhan Sirhan.

Moe: Shakespeare.

Will: Ponce de Leon.

June: Ummm... Caeser.

Moe: Which one?

June: The first one.

Will: Which one was the first one?

June: Julius.

Moe: Oh… well how do you know?

June: Allright, then. Buddha.

Will: Mmmmm… Pol Pot.

Moe: Hey! It was my turn! Ho Chi Minh.

June: Umm… Adolf Hitler.

Will: Adolph Coors.

Moe: Adolf Eichmann.

Will: He dead? Yeah, I guess he would have to be…

Moe: I don't know. Maybe he wasn't. Want me to do another one? Billy the Kid.

June: George Washington.

Will: Washington Irving.

Moe: Peter Stuyvesant.

June: Irving Berlin.

Will: Jerry Garcia.

Moe: Judge Charles J. Vallone.

June: eh… eh… eh… Did you say Archduke Ferdinand?

Will: Yes, I think I did.

June: Huh… Siddhartha.

Moe & Will: You said that!

June: No I didn't!

Will: Yes. Yesyesyes. You said Buddha.

June: Different.

Moe: It isn't.

June: Sure it is.

Will: Well Buddha's not dead, then.

June: All right, all right. I'll pick a different one. Um… Peter Minuit. Sitting Bull. Amelia Earheart.

Will: Joseph Pulitzer.

Moe: Nobel.

June: What was his first name?

Moe: I don't know.

June: You can't do that… Doesn't count, then.

Moe: Bullshit! You can't say Buddha, then. Which Buddha? The Laughing Buddha? The smiling Buddha…

Will: (with an air of superiority) All right ladies, play nice. Its Alfred Nobel. Let's see..Gengis Khan!

June: Marco Polo.
Moe: Hmm…

June: (defensively) It's a natural jump.

Moe: Joan of Ark.

Will: Rasputin. He was also burned at the stake.

June: River Phoenix.

Moe: Shannon Hoon

Will: Bradley Noell.

June: (cattily) I'm sorry, friend of yours?

Will: (hurt) The SUBLIME kid.

Moe: He's dead?

Will: Very.

Moe: How?

Will: I think he Od'd.

June: Kurt Cobain.

Will: Umm...

June: (defensively) Well, you said od'd.

Moe: Yeah, yeah, yeah, shove it up your bum. Let's see now...
Carl Sagan.

Will: Christopher Wren.

June:

Moe: Very nice, very nice...um...Christa Mcaulliff.

June: That's sad...

Moe: Yeah, it's terrible.

June: It really is.... ummm... Chuck Yeager.

Moe: He's not dead, stupid

June: Ha...I do this every time, don't I?

Moe: Yeah, you're an idiot.

June: Now I'll feel really bad when Chuck Yeager does die. Umm...Hans Christian Anderson.

Will: Very good. Jack Ruby.

Moe: Jacob Grimm

June: Aesop

Will: Charles Kuralt.

Moe: Umm...Henry David Thoreau.

June: Mark David Chapman. Actually, wait, he might not be dead.

Will: Pick another.

June: Umm...Groucho Marx.

Will: Karl Marx. That's a given.

Moe: Abraham Lincoln.

June: Nelson Rockefeller.

Will: Hank Aaron

Moe: Fiorello LaGuardia. Fiorello...fiorello...fiorello... fiorello...

June: Princess Diana.

Will: I don't think you're allowed.

June: But she's dead. What difference does it make? Allright, all right, Charles Lindbergh.

Will: Mmmm...Lyndon B. Johnson.

Moe: Rutherford B. Hayes.

June: Grover Cleveland.

Will: Zachary Taylor.

Moe: Mr. Hooper from Sesame Street.

June: I'll take your word on that one.

Moe: He really is dead.

Will: Harry Crews. Oh wait, Harry Crews isn't dead. Frederick Exley, then.

Frederick Exley is dead?

Quite.

When?

1992.

Charles Bukowski.

Umm...let's see...RFK.

Lee Harvey Oswald. I already said Sirhan Sirhan.

Alexander the Great.

Alexander Graham Bell.

Galileo.

Copernicus.

Who's the guy with the fountain of youth?

I think you said him already.

No, I didn't.

You said V...no, no, it was like a Francis...

Nah, it was something with a V. Any way...let me think...think of a good

one...ah, yes, Karen Carpenter.

Janis Joplin.

Mama Cass.

Judy Garland.

Marilyn Monroe.

Thomas Paine.

Thomas Jefferson.

Jacob Beam.

Fuck you.

What you mean, fuck me? He's dead!

Yeah. And that's a good thing.
Um...John Daniels.

Alfred J. Titslinger.

Daniel Webster. And it's Otto J. Titslinger, isn't it?

Otto. Yeah, you're right. Henry Clay.

Henry Ford.

Ford Maddox Ford.

John Wilkes Booth.

<in between scene...walk to or from roof. three people (undetermined) smoking on landing>

Person 1: "We've got the american jesus...tiny voices...i want to conquer the world...classics...i didn't discover them until after the millenium, and its been a real treat...like a long distance dedication from 1992. Which is weird, because all my other stories start or end in 1987."

Person 2: "You're missing my point...you can't view ostensibly political material without the necessary context in which it was written. Ten years later...and you're just pavlovs dog, salivating to the right chords."

Person 3: "Uh...listen, buddy...i think that he was just saying that it rocked. So cool it."

Person 1: "Fuckin A."

<other in between scene, same location, person 3, staring and smoking, voiceover>

"I just realized the other day the one thing that brave new world and 1984 got wrong. They didn't have to force us to become each others keeper, and turn over every nearly aspect of our daily lives to the hive...we went willingly to this ironic death. we gleefully monitor each others private and public lives for the slightest crack of inappropriate or questionable behaviour. WE LIKE the new world order. didn't they do blue monday...bizarre love triangle?" fades out.

<yet another in between scene>

Captain Mike walks by ams office, does something a little odd...after he passes:

Angry young woman: "Who the hell was that guy, and what the hell is his problem?"

Man: "Hey, that's Captain Mike. He's a Veteran...got a Purple Heart in Desert Storm...have a little respect."

Scene 7: The Roof

- more arguing - quick flash to office where person 3 is still at computer. Zoom in on little envelope. Back to roof for "Its time."

June: I got another one of those e-mails today about those kidney harvesters in New Orleans. That's so fucking sick.

Will: Yup.

June: I mean, here you are in some dive bar and you meet the man of your dreams and he up and steals your kidney. What's up with that?

Will: Maybe it's just a fetish.

June: No way. They're making tons of money off it. It's barbaric.

Will: (amused and condescending) You know none of that shit's true. It's all just an urban legend, like that thing about the microwaves and the exploding glass.

June: I don't know. It could be true. Kidneys are worth a lot of money to some people. I know a guy who was on dialysis for months. I bet he would have paid a lot for a kidney.

Will: Maybe you should have sold him one instead of coming to me.

June: Maybe.

Will: Do you think this is going to work?

June: Probably.

Will: What if it doesn't work?

June: 'S no skin off my back. You two need it more than I do.

Will: What if we get caught?

June: Mo's guy is good. We won't get caught.

Will: (looks suspicious) How can you be so confident we won't get caught when half an hour ago you were freaking out because a volleyball fell out the window?

June: That was different. That wasn't a part of the plan. We followed the plan. We won't get caught.

Will: Where are you going to go... after?

June: I don't know. Tijuana. Cayman Islands. Someplace warm. Someplace with a beach. And less smog. Maybe Burkina Faso. Help Mo's Uncle Ed set up his gambling racket. You?

Will: Kathmandu. Nepal. I'm going to get me a Sherpa guide and climb Mount Everest. Know why? Because its there.

June: Sounds... cold.

Will: Not in the sun.

I think they should throw something else off the roof here, for continuity.

Quick cut to Mo at the computer. The little outlook mail symbol is there. Next shot is Will and June looking over the side of the roof. The door opens.

Mo: Its time.

Snack Foods

Want to come with us?

No, I'm cold.

Go sit on the radiator...it'll warm you up.

It's not even on. It's cold.

Yeah, I know..it's a problem. We're working on it...

1

Button up the coat against the cold. Early morning sun hurts.
Shades drawn. 25 days now? 50? No. That party last
Tuesday. Woohoo.

Friendly coffee ladies. Smile.

Peer out the window of the Dunkin Donuts®. Clear sailing.

Nearly spilling. Through the door of the building. Nice high
ceilings. Horror at the ambience. Smile to the people, nod at
the headstones. Up in the old Otis®.

4th Floor. Happy Media®.

2

Reception Area. 4 Offices. Plus the Big Space. Nice. Time to
see what disasters have befallen us today.

CNNDAILYNEWSPRESSDRUDGETIMESESPN.

What day is it?

3

Todo:

Fix Daily Examiner main page
   Email Server
Update Client Links
Call Kenyon
   SONY/Canon

Meet with SCI, Berklay
Romeo & Juliet Rehearsals
Pay Sprint Bill

Check the e and voice. No news. Good news. Gobble it down.

4. The quiet joys. Music in the Big Space. Long view. Steel oneself for the day.

2 Scenes from "In Medias Res"

(a play)

Scene 1

"It's not a good idea to put your wife into a novel; not your latest wife anyway." Norman Mailer

(Man and woman walking slowly down city street, late one evening. Radiohead's How I Made Millions is playing in the Dive Bar they pass. They reach a corner.)

He: Where are we going?

She: Well, I'm going home.

He: As well you should. Good night.

She: I'll walk you to your door.

He: Ok.

(They continue walking. It is very late, and their steps echo heavily on the wet pavement. The slowly walk a half block. Arriving at a nondescript doorway, they stop and kiss.)

He: Do you want to come up?

She: No.

(Kisses him. A rare pedestrian walks by, so they move from the middle of the sidewalk to up against the concrete wall of the building.)

She: So does it bother you when I flirt with the other guys?

He: Not in the least.

She: Tell me why not?

(He pauses...shakes his head slowly, grimly, from side to side. The answer comes back to him "Well, you seem like a cool, smart, sexy girl. But I hardly know you. And only a real nut would be jealous at this stage." He laughs a little.)

He: Um...that's between you and me.

She: Why are you laughing? And it's 4:30 in the morning. We're the only ones out here.

He: Shut up.

(He kisses her)

He: Sure you don't want to come up?

She: Yeah...I'm sure.

He: Well then call me tomorrow. Do you have my cell phone number?

She: No. Are you going to write it on one of your big yellow pieces of notebook paper?

He: I just might.

(She leans in and kisses him.)

He: Ah...nevermind. Nighty-nite.

(She starts to walk away.)

He: Hey...what's *your* number?

(She turns her head, still walking.)

She: You. Don't. Have it.

(She shakes it for all she's worth down the block. He watches her until she's out of sight. Shakes his head slowly, leans up against the same wall, and lights a cigarette.)

Scene 5

(7:45 on a Saturday night. A brooding young man walks into a fairly crowded bar. He sees several familiar faces, and slowly walks towards the end. Nearing his usual stool, he notices a quiet, unfamiliar guy down near his usual seat, next to a cake with candles. A look around, and behind the bar, brings a quick, guilty grin and a look of recognition across his face.)

Irish Guy midway down the bar: And how is our boy today?
Big Girl a few seats down: Yes, what can you tell us?
He: I'm...well. As I hope you both are. And I think I'm going to move over there next to you two, where there's a bit more room.

(He smiles, and slowly walks towards an empty stool between the two. He takes his seat, as the barmaid approaches.)

She: So, do you want your whiskey?
He: Yes. Better yet, how about 7 or 8. Just line them right up.

(She pours his drink, then walks to the front of the bar. He drinks a gulp of the bourbon, then slowly shakes his head and smiles, lighting a cigarette.)

IG: So what is your secret, good sir. What ails thee.
He: There is no secret, and nothing ails me. I'm living the dream, every day.
IG: Indeed. We should all feel the same way. Though from the look of that gentleman in your seat, not all of us do.

(Barmaid walks down the length of the bar, towards the end. The Irish fellow holds his arm out to stop her, and gestures towards the young man.)

IG: Get this man a drink, will you.
She: He's still got some. And I know he likes to nurse these things.

(He gulps down the rest of the drink, and gently slams the rocks glass down)

He: And may I please have a glass of water. I am trying, against all odds, to remain properly hydrated.

(She pours the whiskey, and places it in front of him. She walks back over to the gun, and deliberately pours ice and water into another glass, and places it front of him. The conversation begins again around them. She looks away, and walks down towards the end of the bar.) Not long thereafter, the barmaid fills a glass with ice and soda, and once again places the glass in front of him. She begins to walk away...)

He: What the hell is this?

She: I know you sometimes drink it with your whiskey. And I accidentally poured it for some guy over there. So I figured you might want it.

(She looks at him for a moment, raises her eyebrows, and slowly walks back down towards the end of the bar.)

Endwords

Well, where to begin. At the beginning of this past summer (2006), I added a throwaway "Coming Soon" feature to Weekly Update about Choragus. We do this all the time, and only some of the time do we wind up furthering development of that property.

Choragus has been the brand we used to designate Content Provision Services (writing, editing, and aggregation). In other words, it was the line on a client invoice that we used to describe those sort of services.

Anyway, the teaser ran throughout the Summer, promising that, as you can see on the next page, work was being done. Wasn't the truth, necessarily, but I like the picture. And need something so fill space in the newsletter. After 195 of the damn things, it's sometimes awful hard to motivate properly.

So, the first few days of September come about, and what do you know…it comes to me. Without much deliberate thought…it became clear that it was time for Choragus to become Happy Media's new Print Media Imprint. Later on, I decided to take the plunge myself. It seemed more likely to entertain than, say, an entire book of highlights from Daily Examiner, or something to that effect.

So here it is. I'm more pleased with it than I imagined I might be…mostly because that vast majority of what you've just read or skimmed is genuinely new material. With the exception of my Notes and the Unfinished Works, which are, of course, my favorite of the bunch. Go figure.

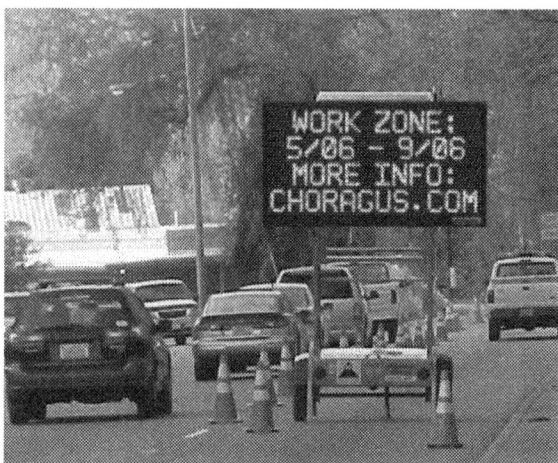

A brief note on the passing of Jack

Just around the time I was starting this project, I went outside to wish my new neighbor, Jack, good luck on the surgery he was to have the next day. It was something structural to do with his neck, and he had been uncertain as to how best to proceed. Well, we heard over the weekend that on Friday, after successful surgery, he had stopped breathing, and gone into intensive care. He was due to have a Brain Scan on Monday. We could tell by the stream of cars on Tuesday that it hadn't gone well. And today, just now in fact, his wife Jean, also a great new neighbor, called to tell us what we already knew.

I share this only to illustrate that, above and beyond anything I'd like to convey within this book-length conversation, you just never know what's around the corner. In the week or two prior to his surgery, my wife and I both remember hearing him say, repeatedly, 'You play the cards you're dealt."

12.27.2006 11:39 PM

Jack's words were the last of this book for quite some time. Maybe 2 months or more. But he wouldn't have wanted it that way, so with a tip of the cap over the hedge we'll move on, and wrap this up.

So here I am, Counselor, working another 12 hour day and counting. Ten years later. Right now I'm cleaning up and finishing this book, while working on the second week of some remarkably explosive development on our Registrant.org, and handling the usual flotsam associated with running a business.

VH1's I Love the 90's: 1997 is about to be on the tv in the background, which, along with the rapidly approaching New Year, has me thinking about how things are different in the world than they were when this whole Happy Media thing started. And how much we've accomplished as a company. But mostly, my mind is occupied, as ever, with the middle to long distance. The big picture. I just order myself a pair of High-Powered Astronomy Binoculars, with which I intend to take advantage of these late nights to attempt to gain a clearer picture of the world.

The Author

Success to us has always been about not having to listen to anybody, and doing whatever what we want to do, and not having to have a day job. Everything else was gravy on top of it, you know? - jack white

Born in New Jersey in 1975, Happy Media Executive Director A.M. Sherwin has been the guiding force behind the company since 1997. He works 7 days a week. Prior to co-founding Happy Media in 1997, Adam wrote for a variety of popular, unpopular, and trade publications (including the NY Daily News and The Berkshire Record), and worked as a dishwasher, salesman, telemarketer, temp, video store manager, waiter, and pet shop boy.

Adam is available for analysis and consultation on projects relating to corporate naming, community stewardship, and media. He'd like to thank his wife, the Wins and Sherwins, the LaRoses, and the Smiths.

He is represented by Author's Agent Representation (www.authorsagent.com).

CHORAGUS

Volume 2: Heavy Static

January 2008